SOCCER SPLENDOR

A Coloring Adventure on the Pitch

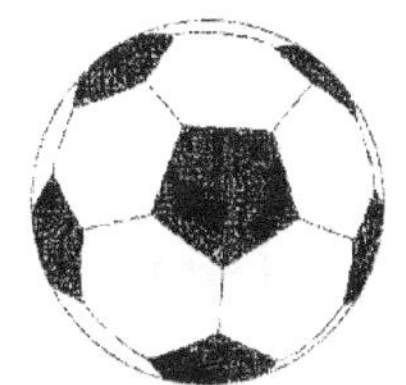

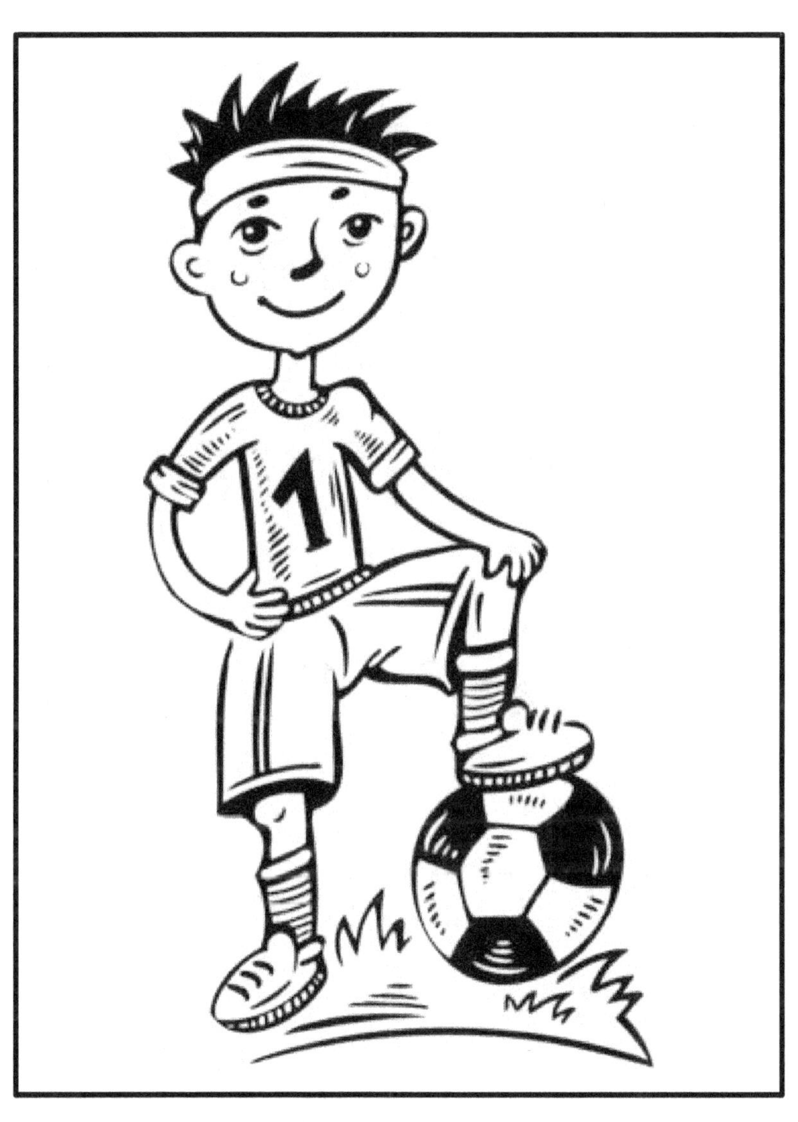

Hello my friend! Let's go on a coloring adventure!

I will leave a blank

page after each

picture for you to

write or draw

whatever you like!

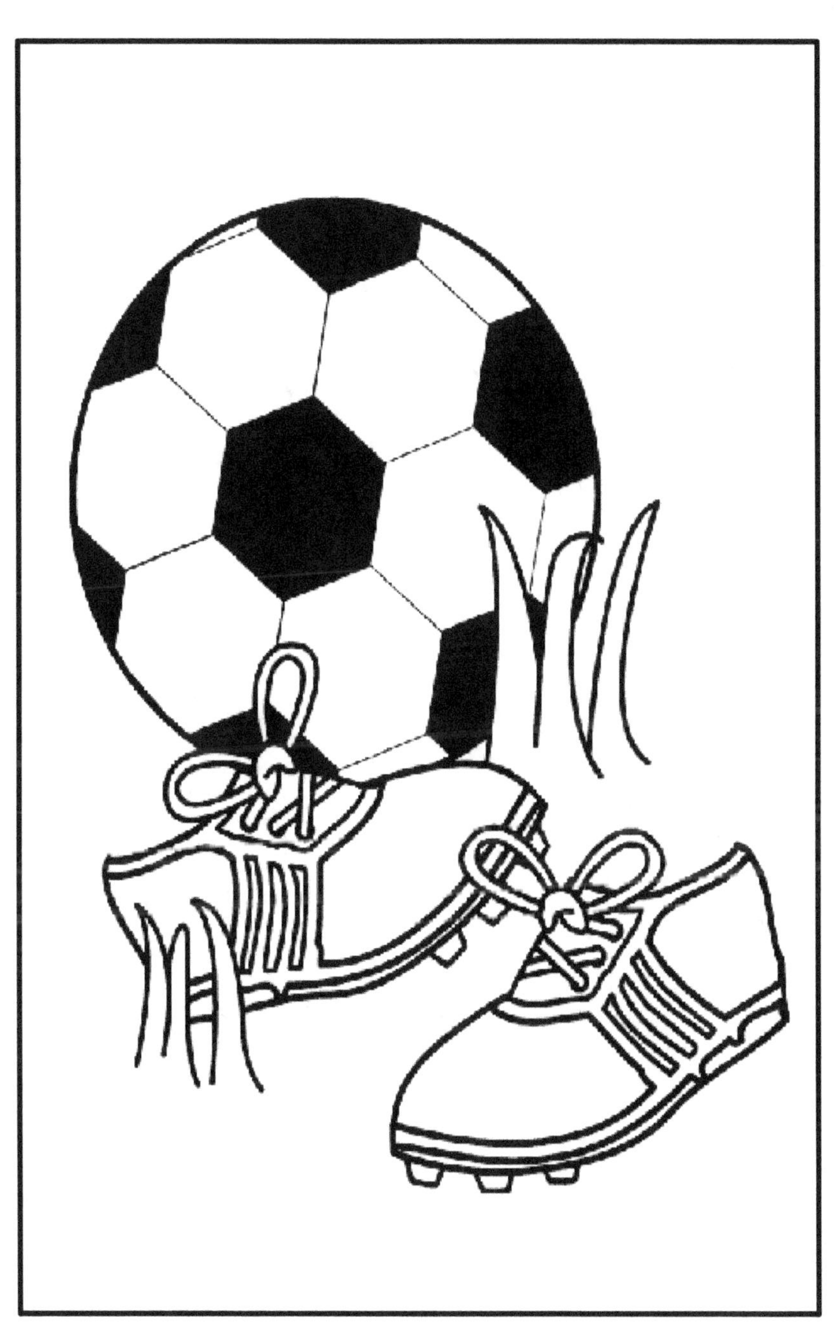

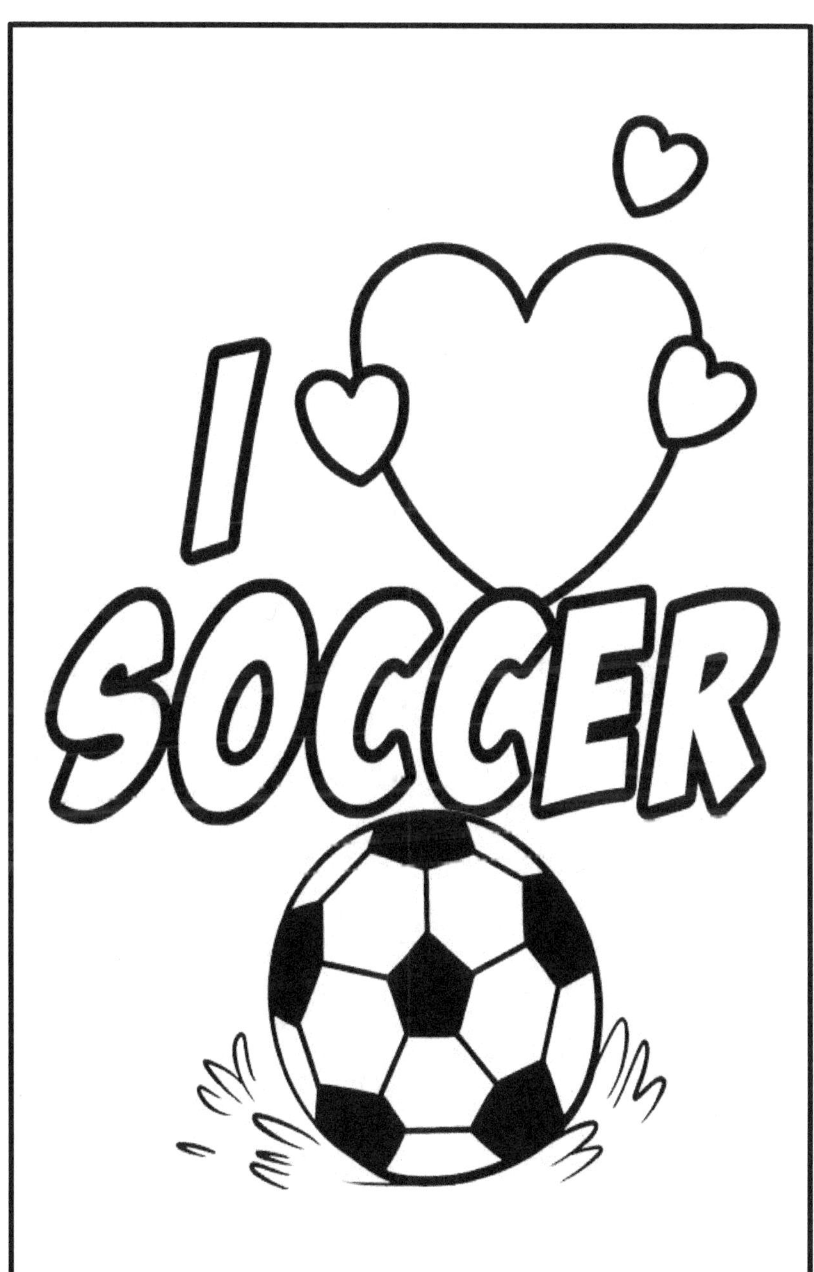

I ♥
SOCCER

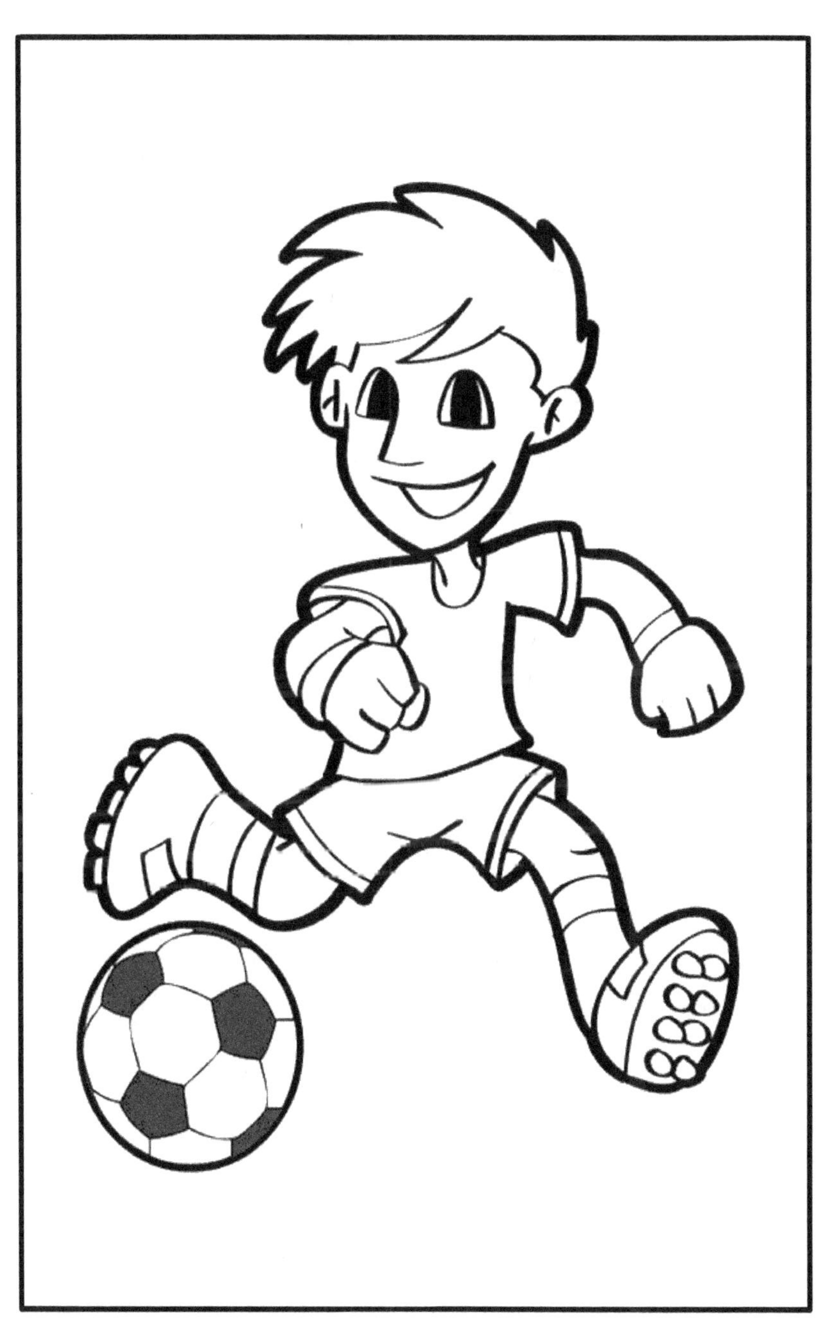

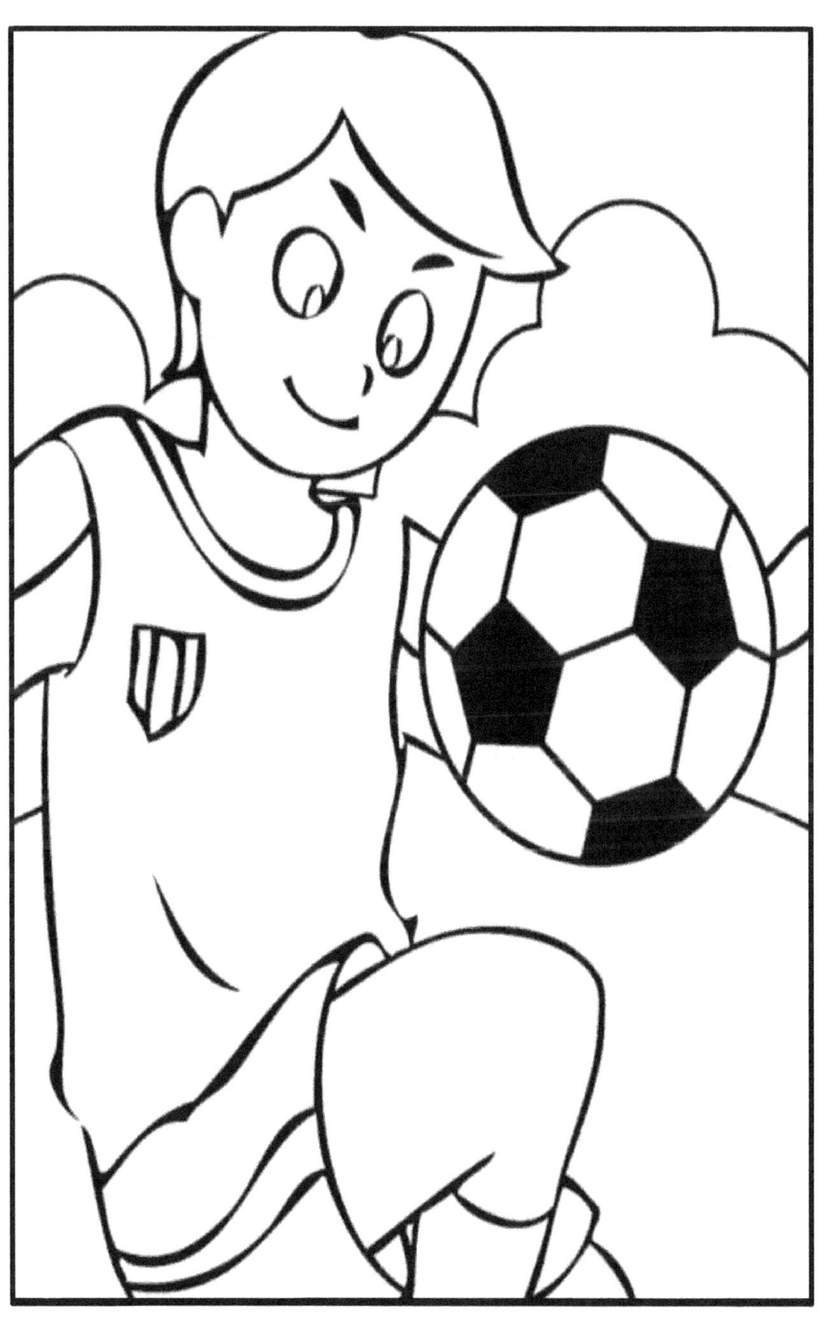

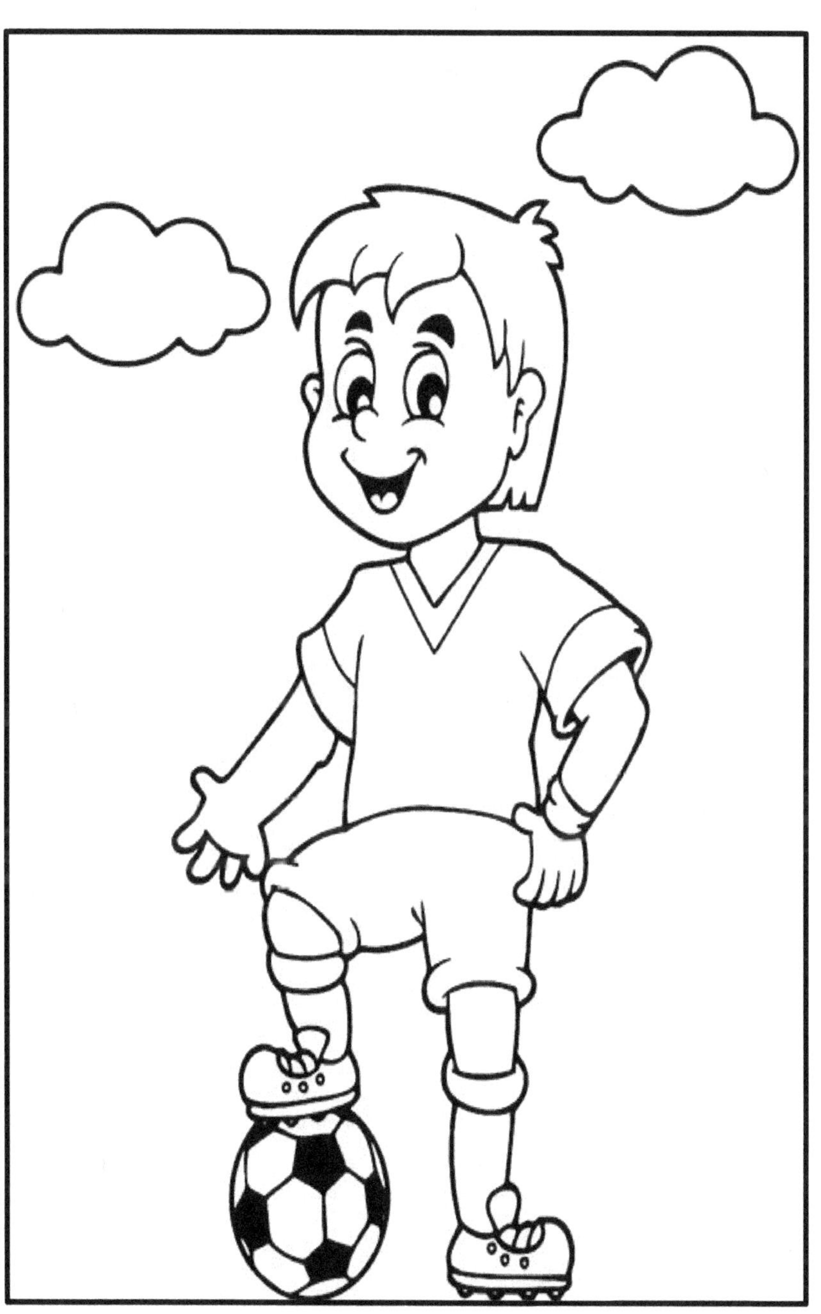

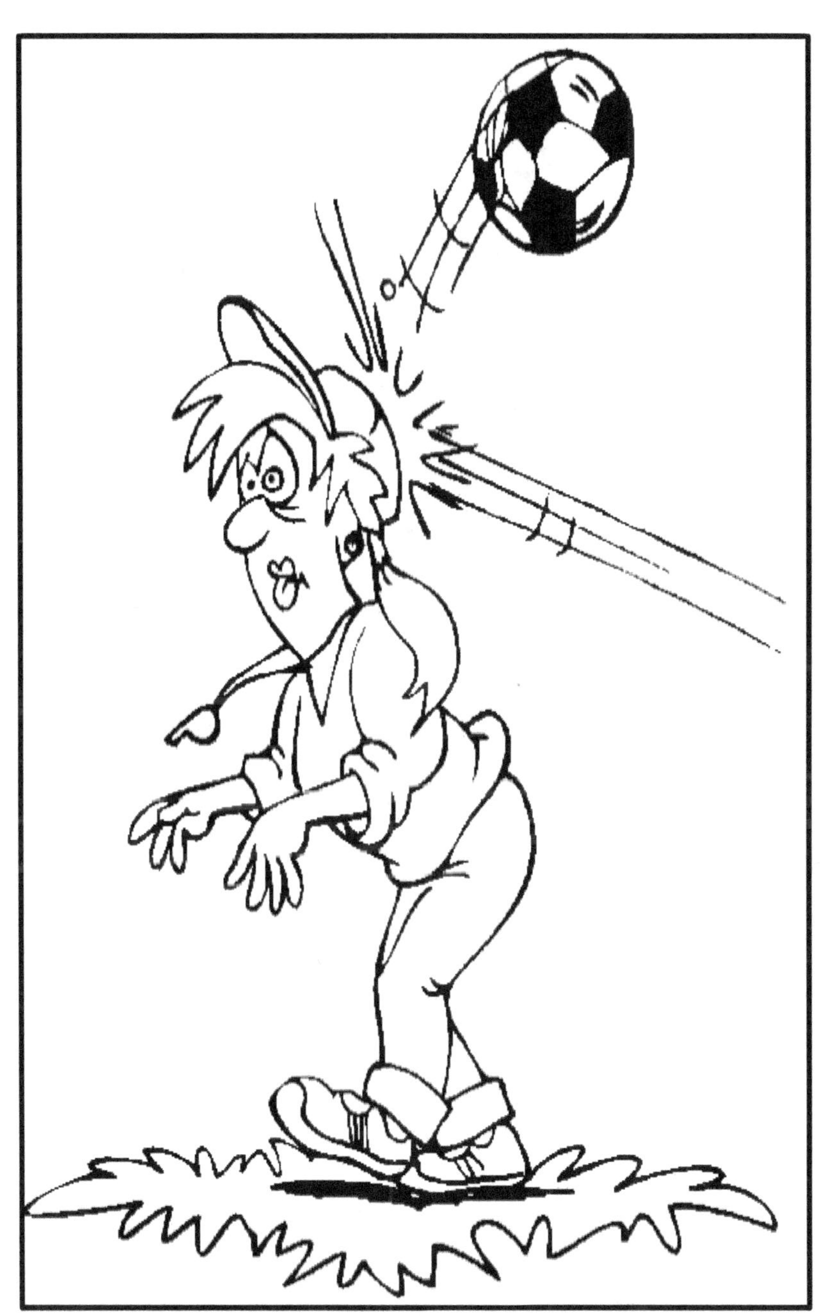

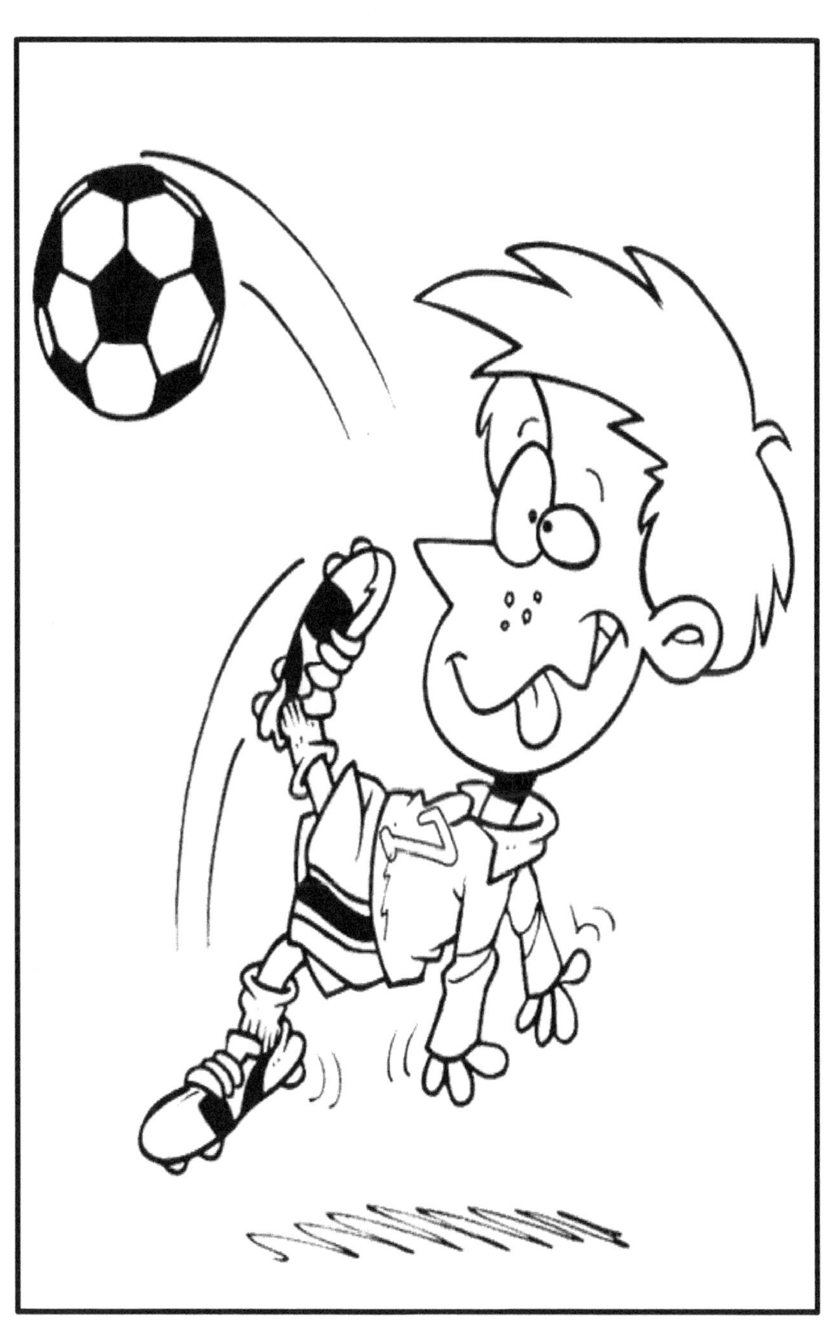

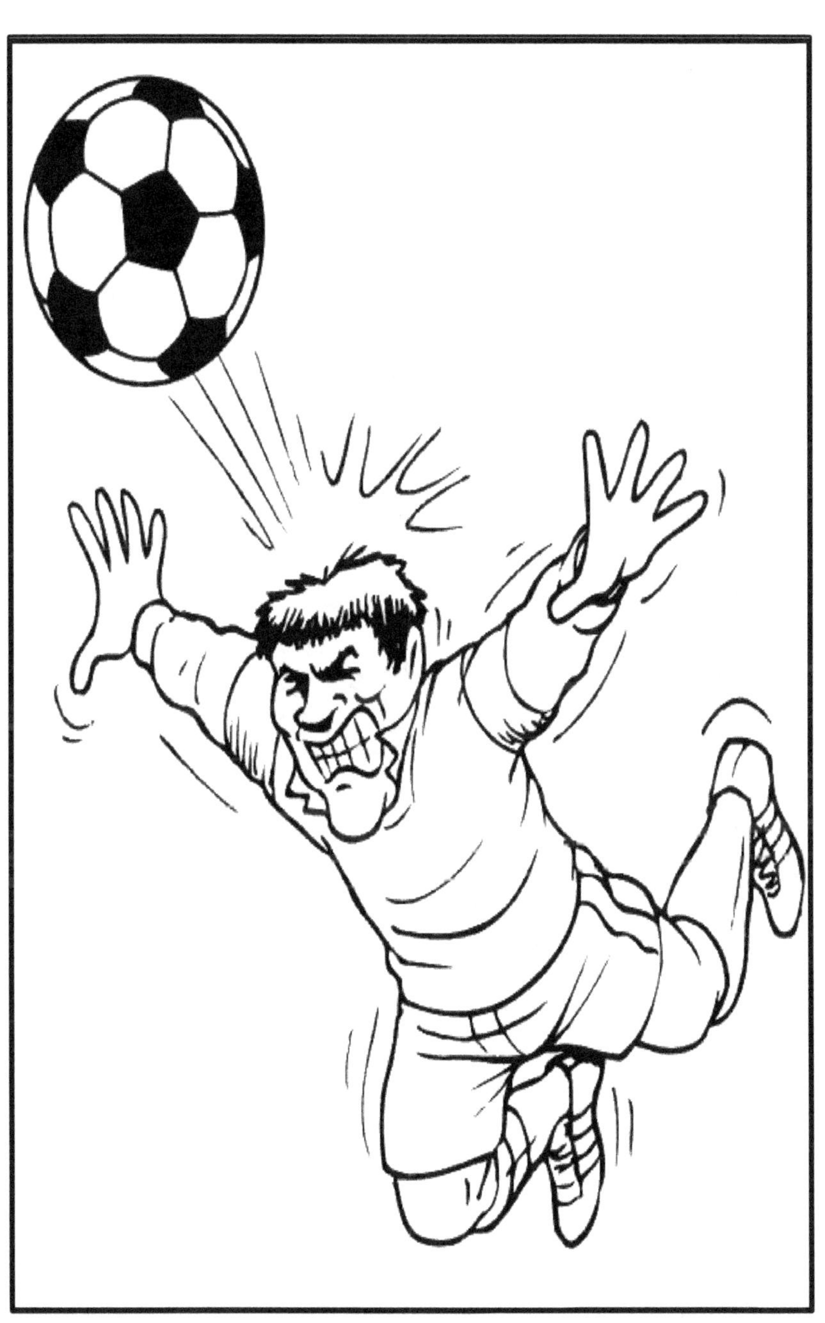

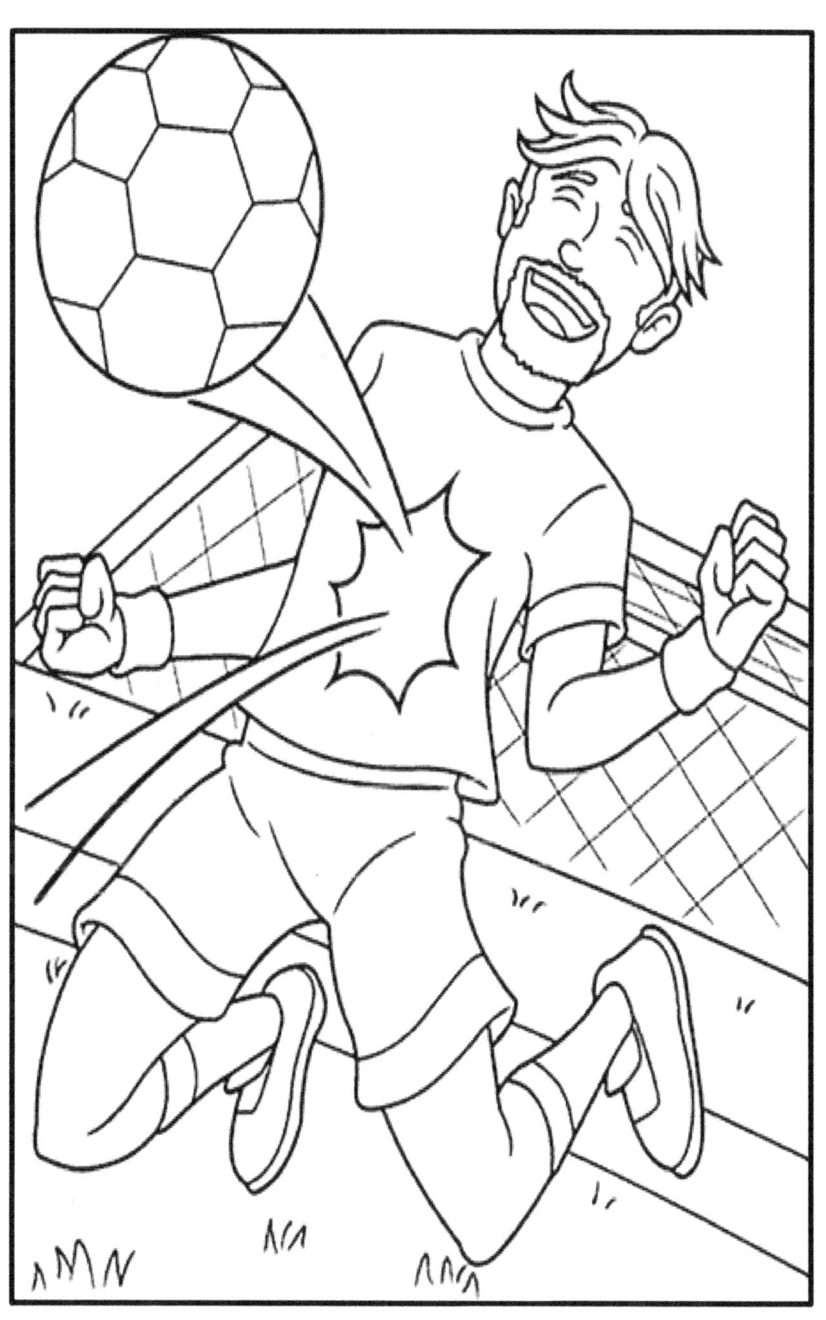

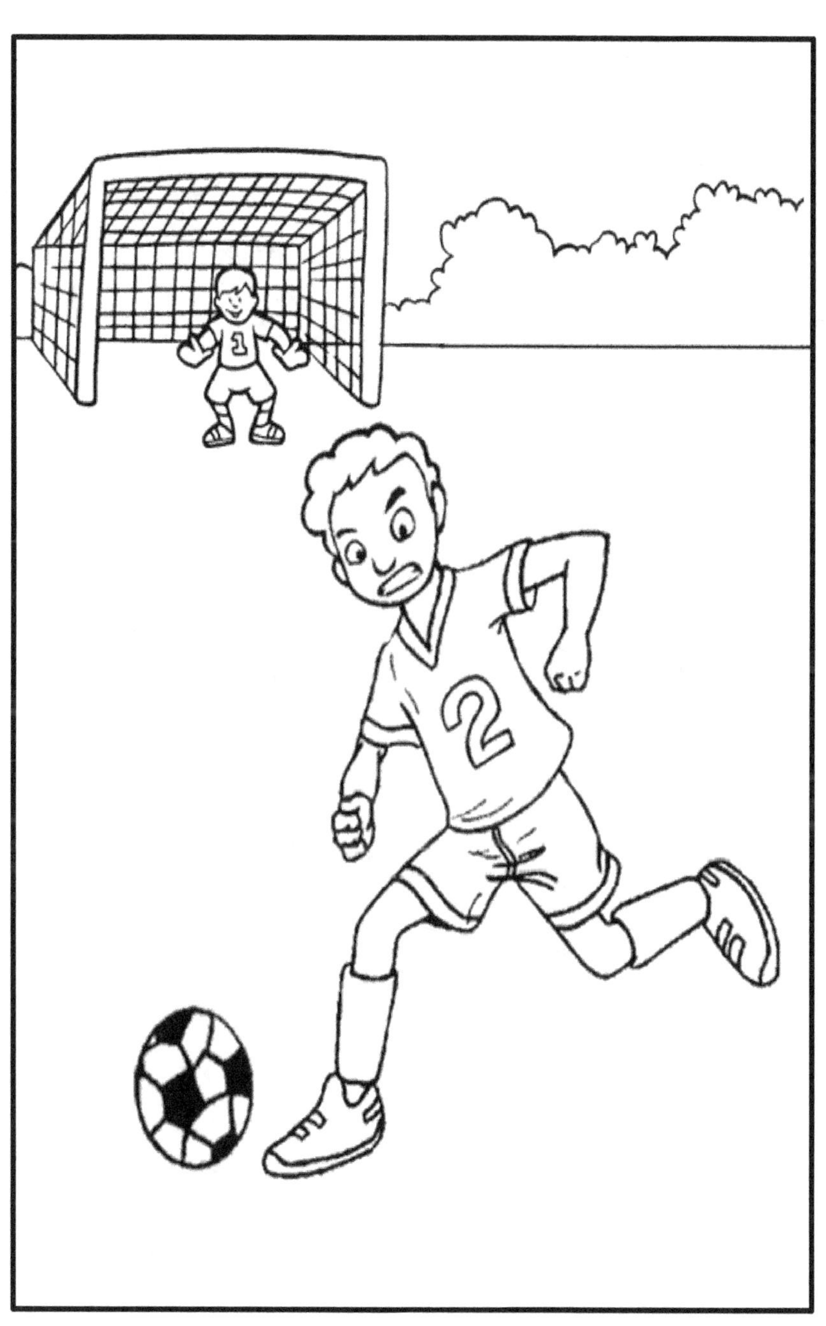

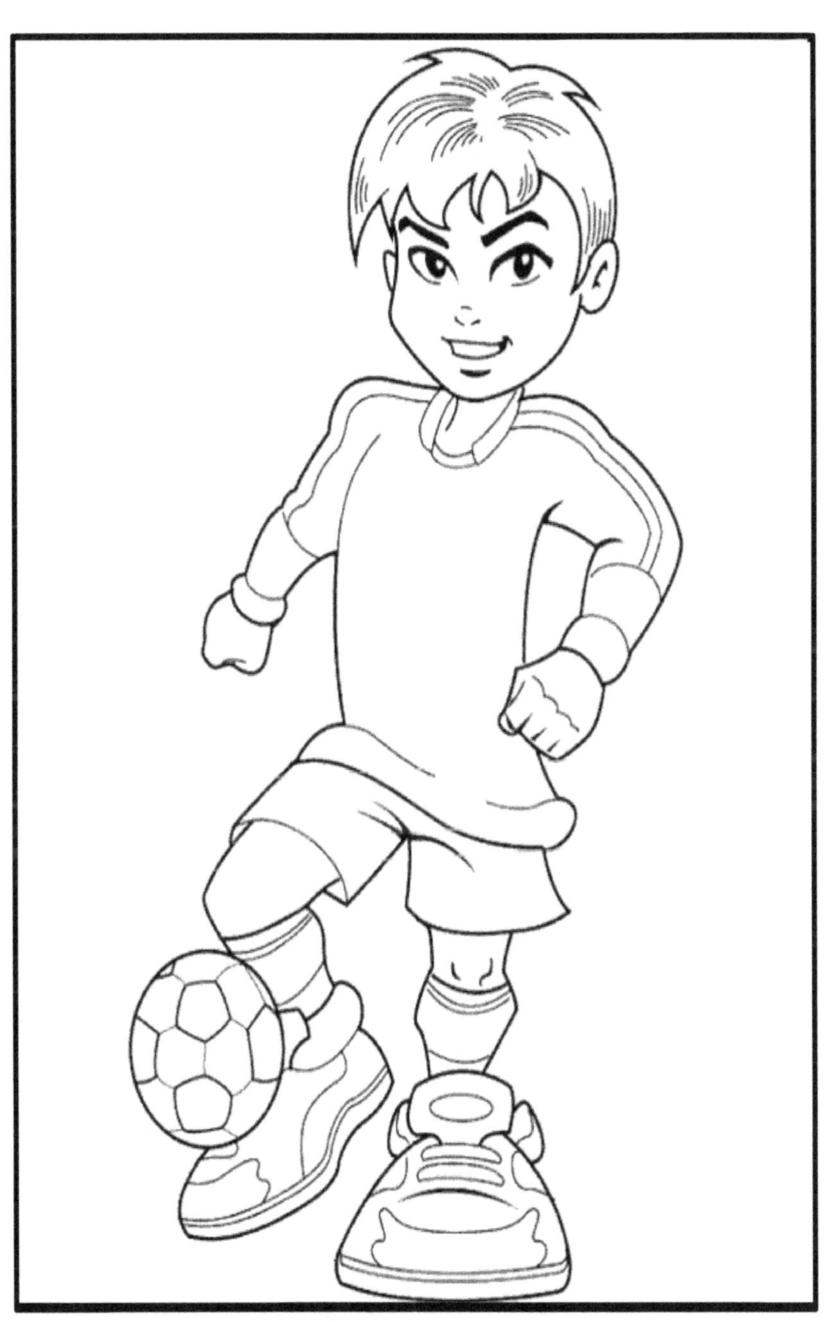

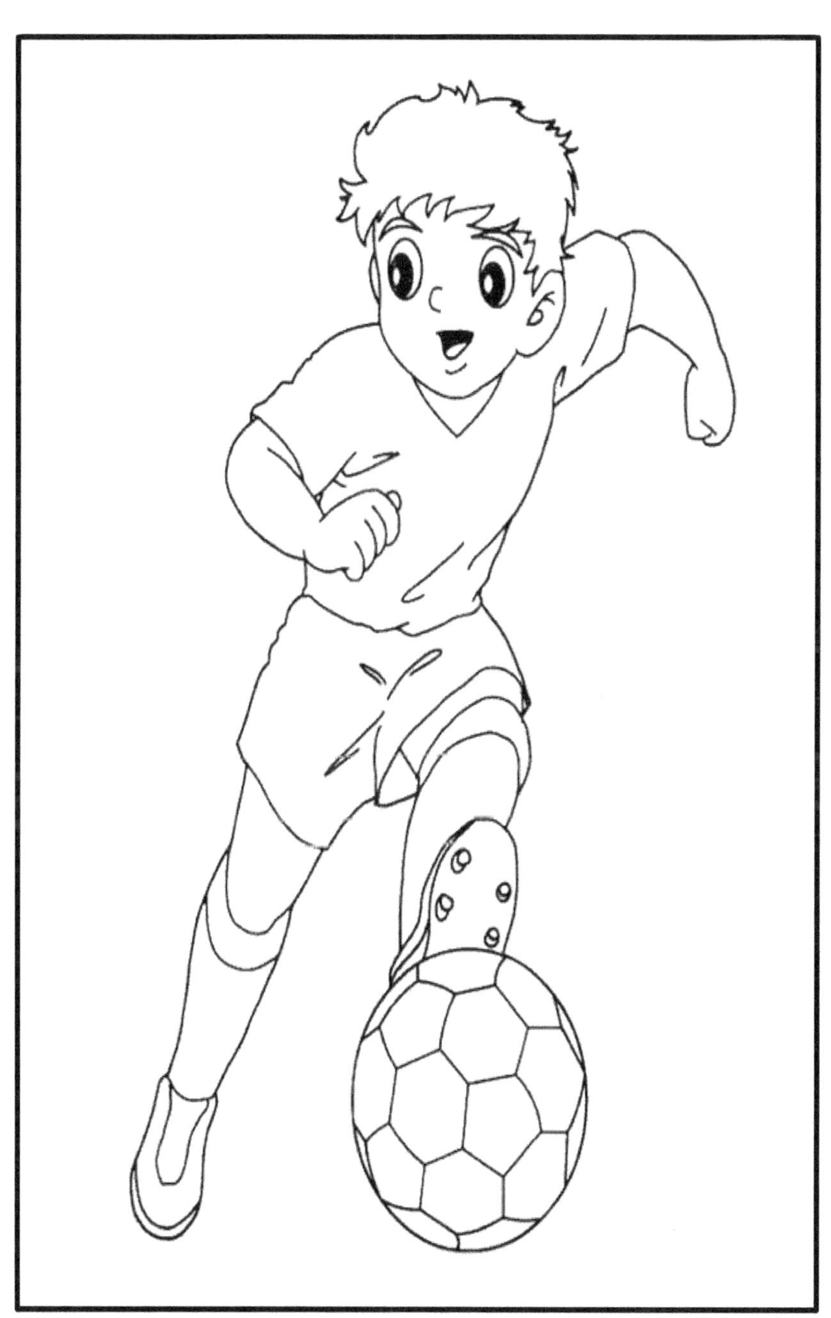

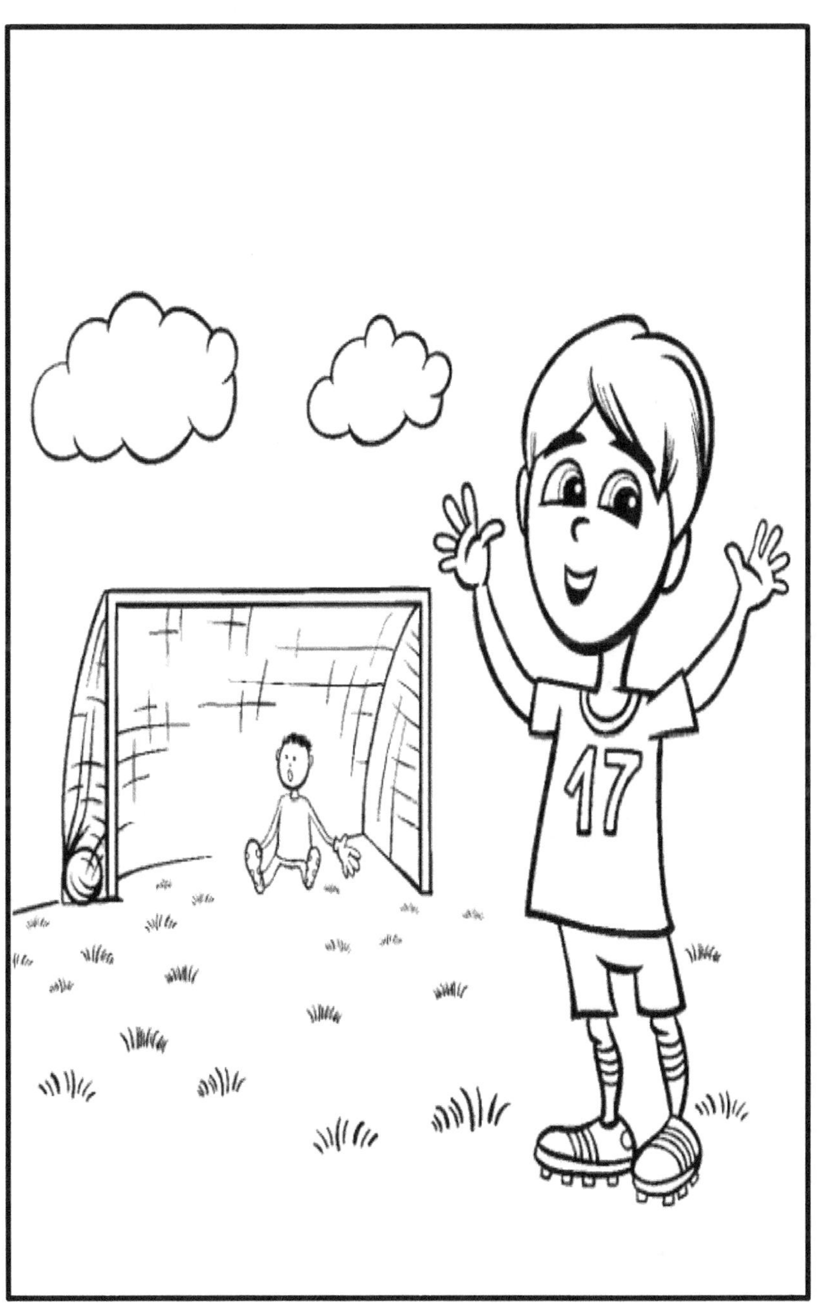

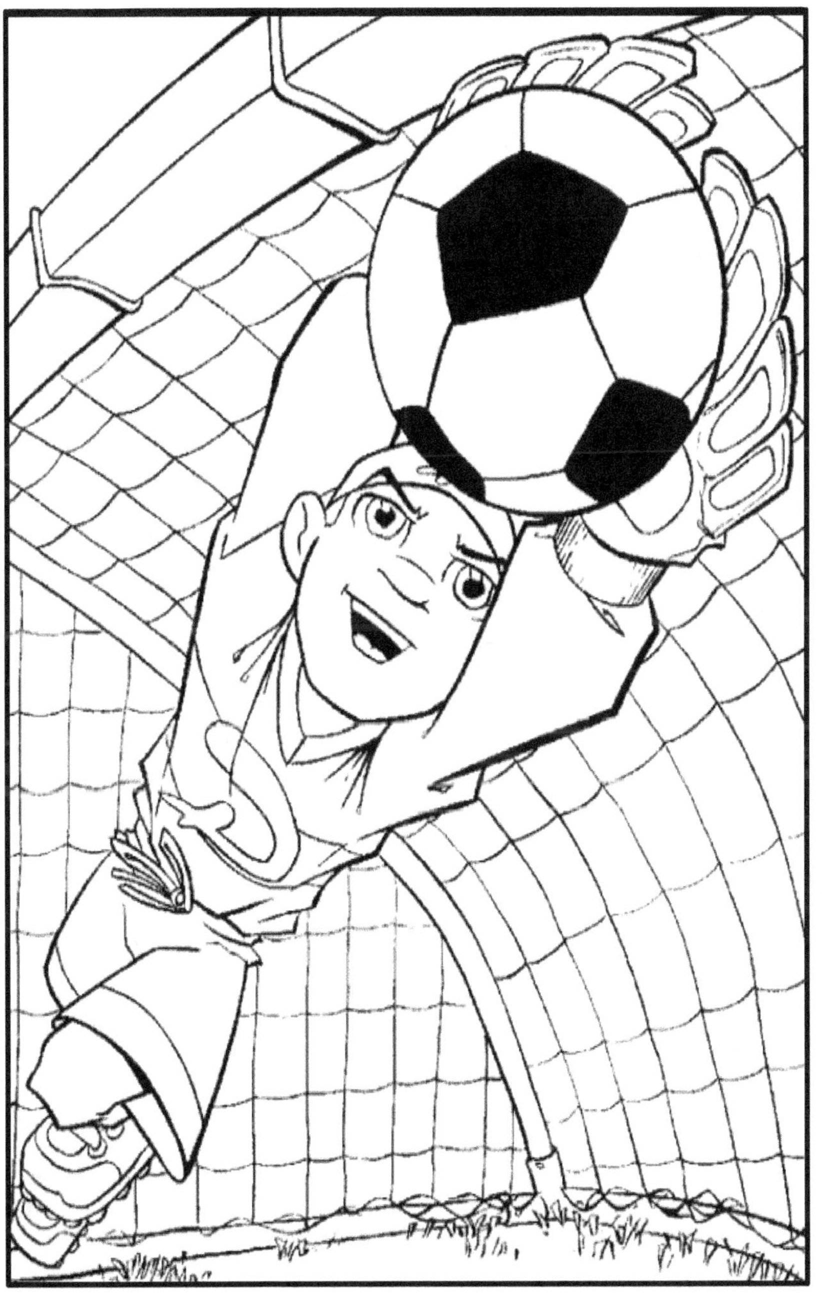

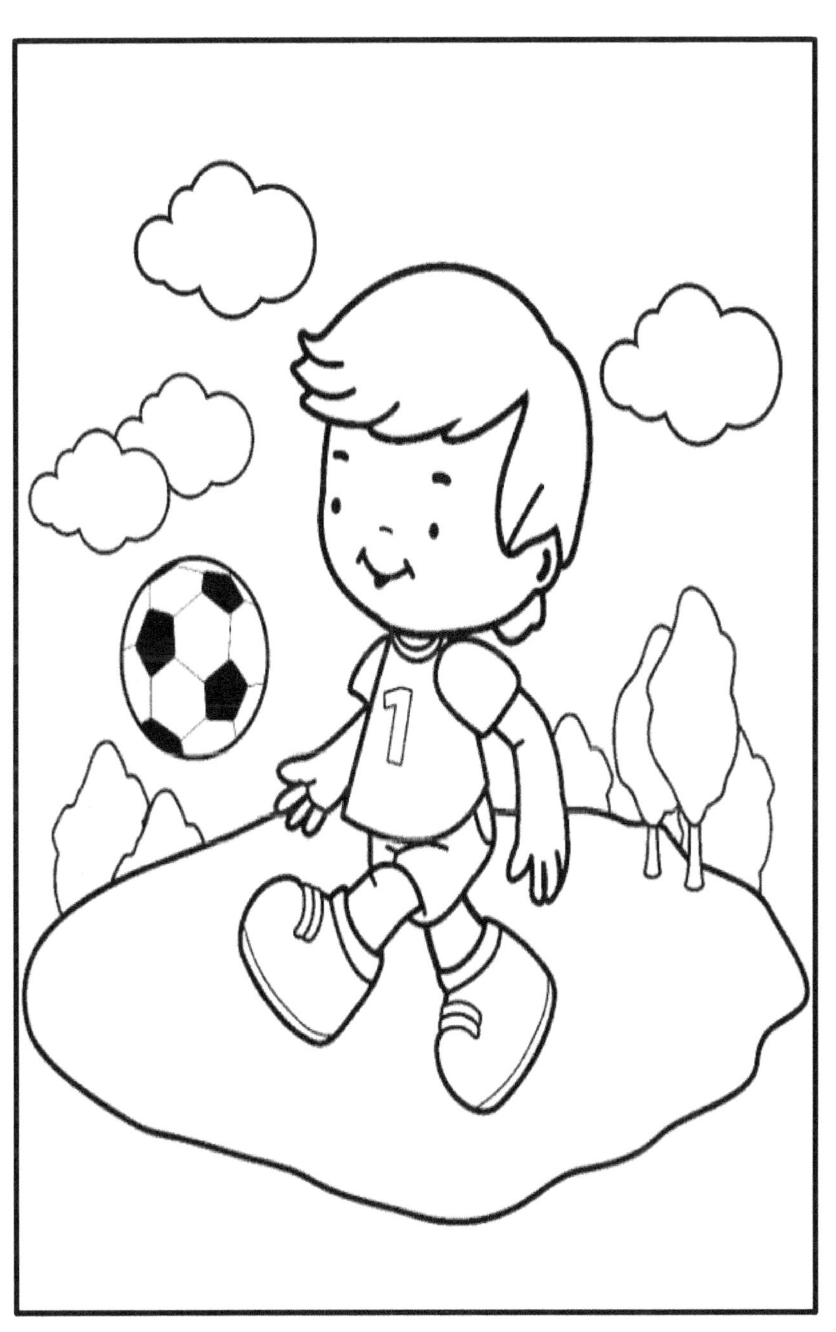

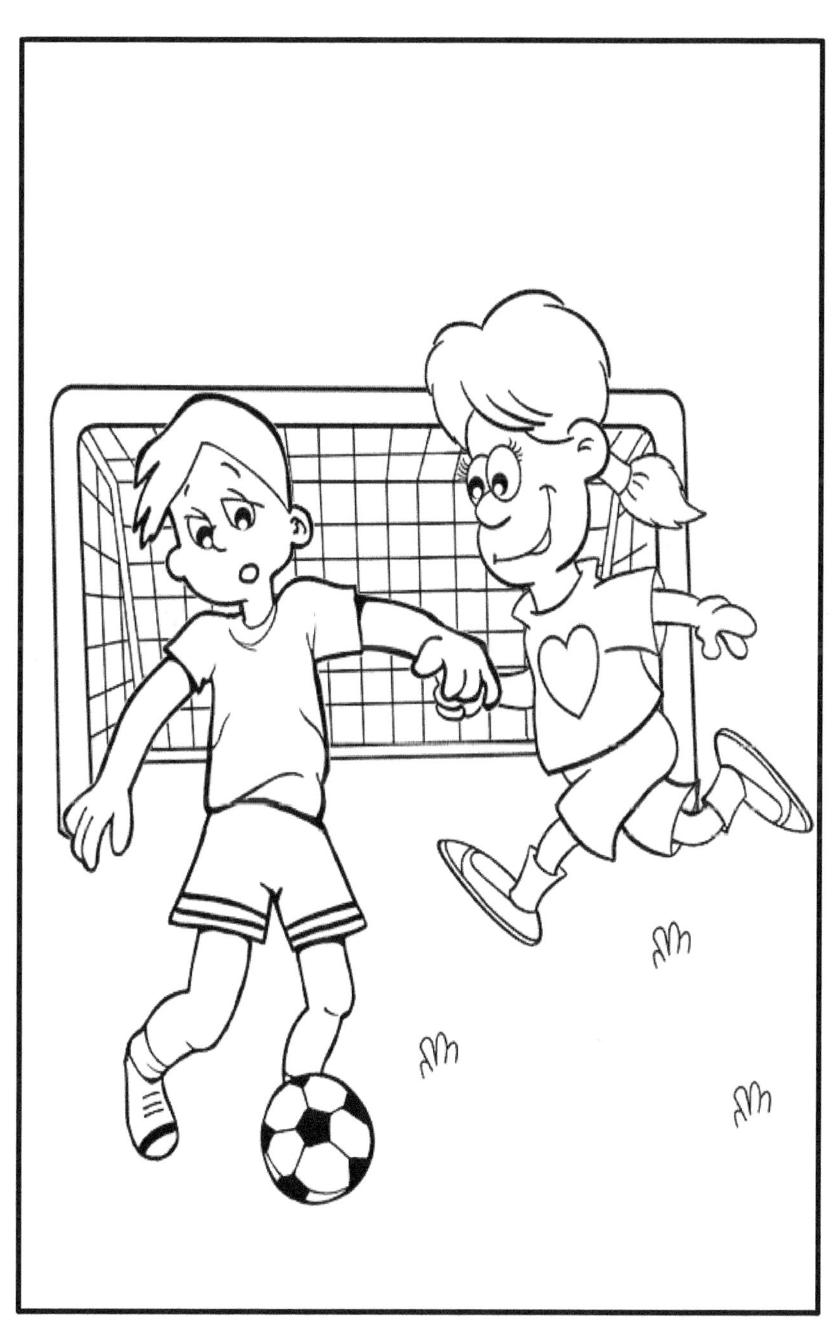

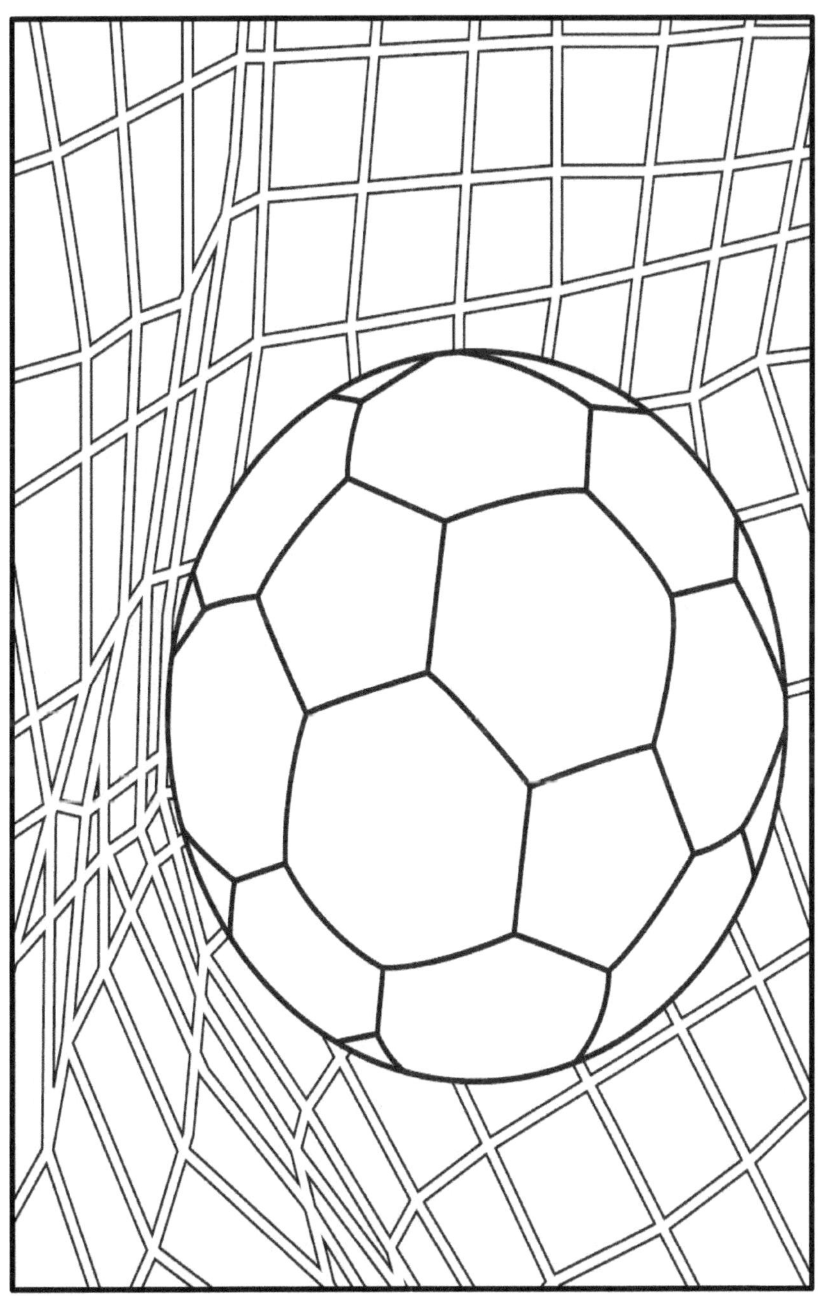

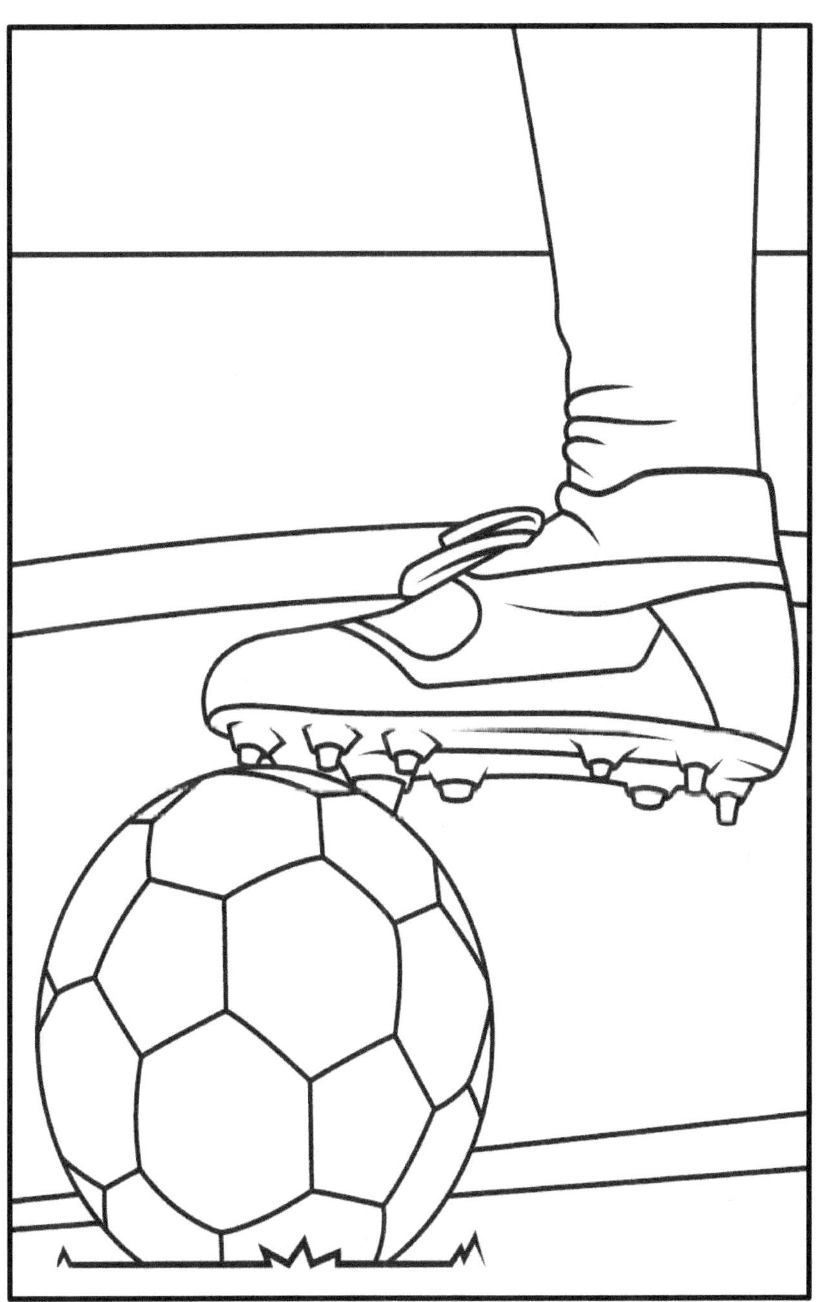

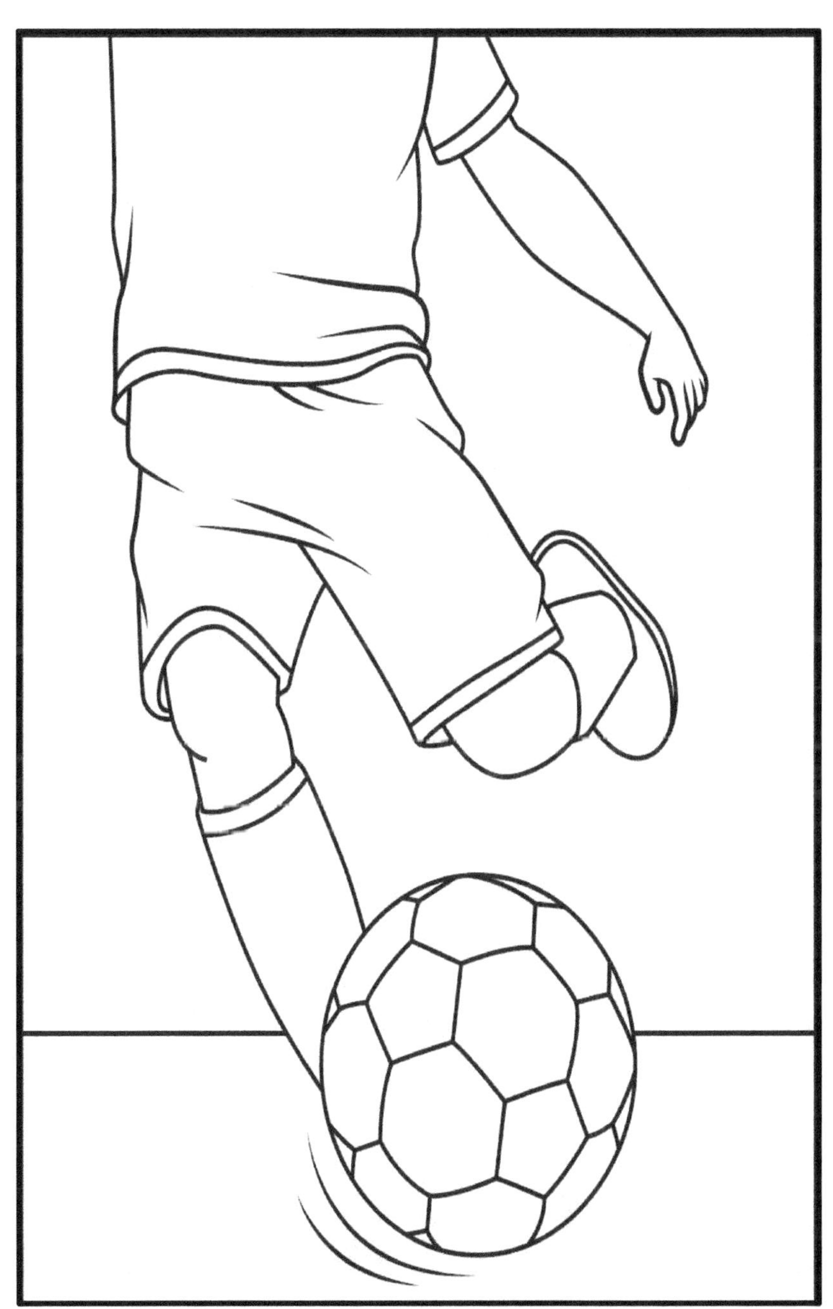

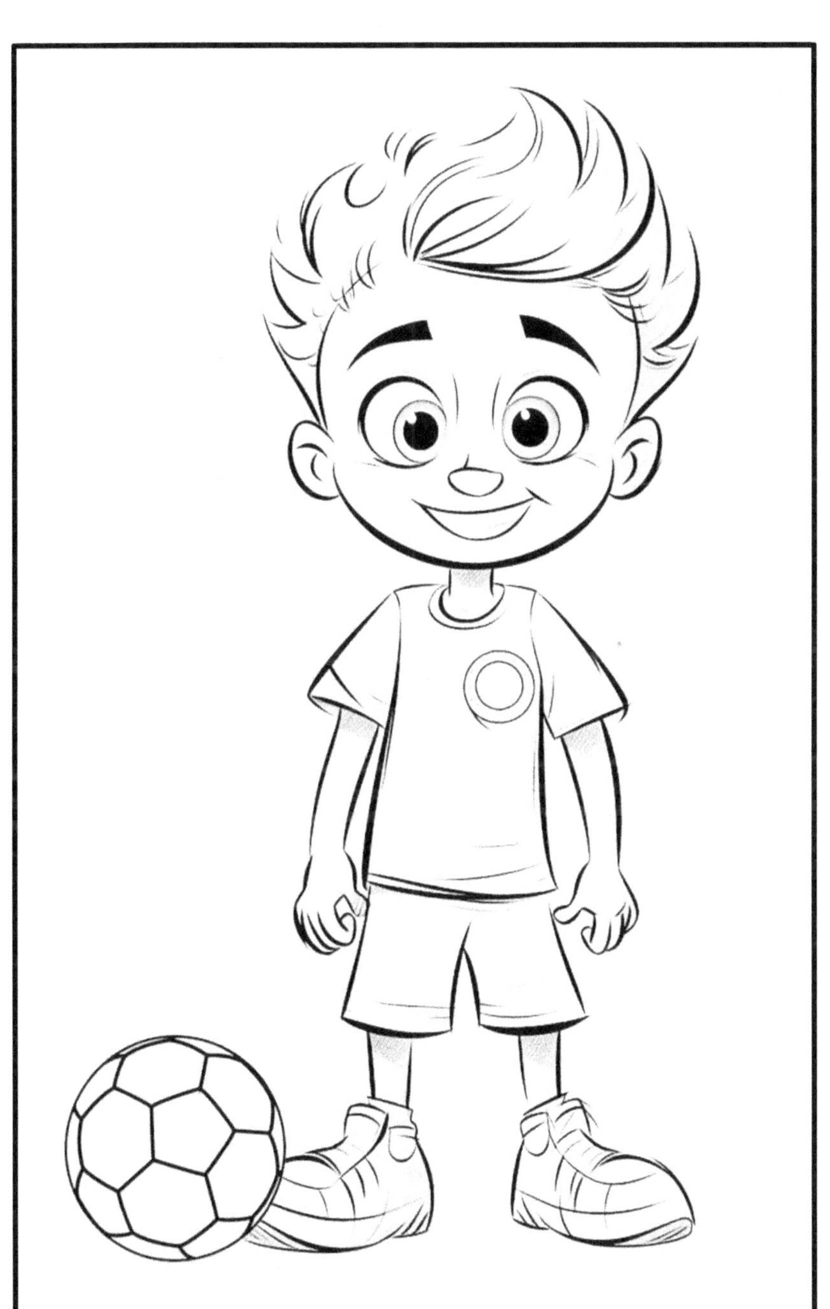

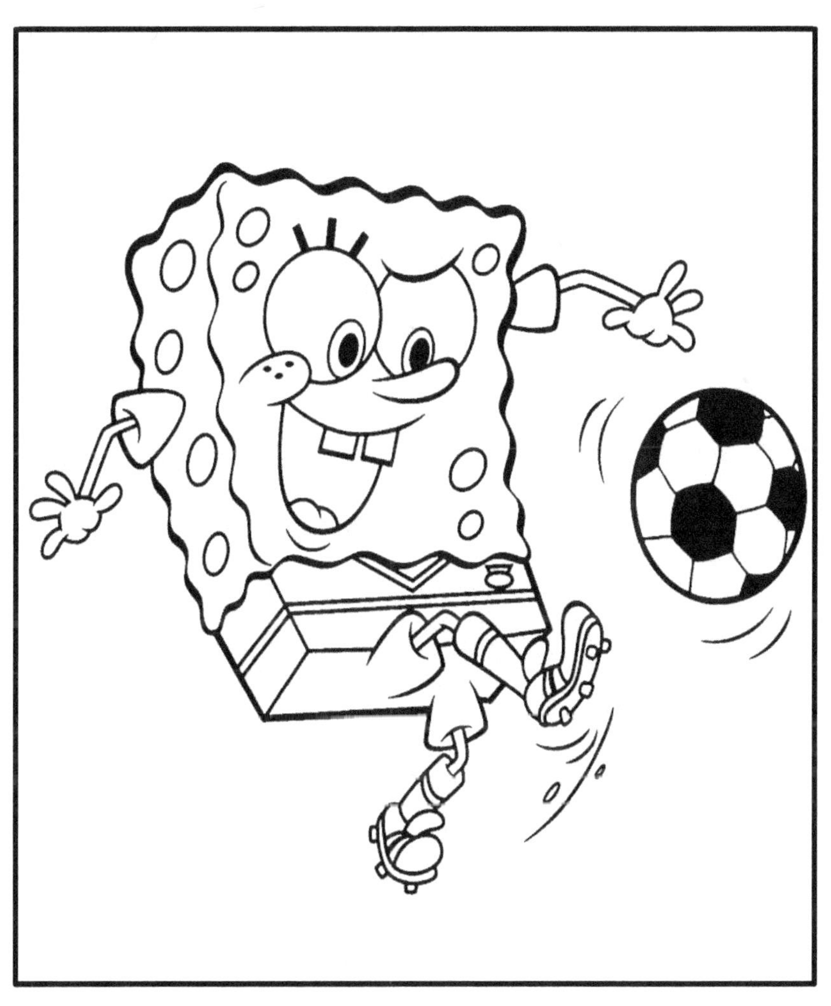

Do you want spongebob to be on

your team?

....

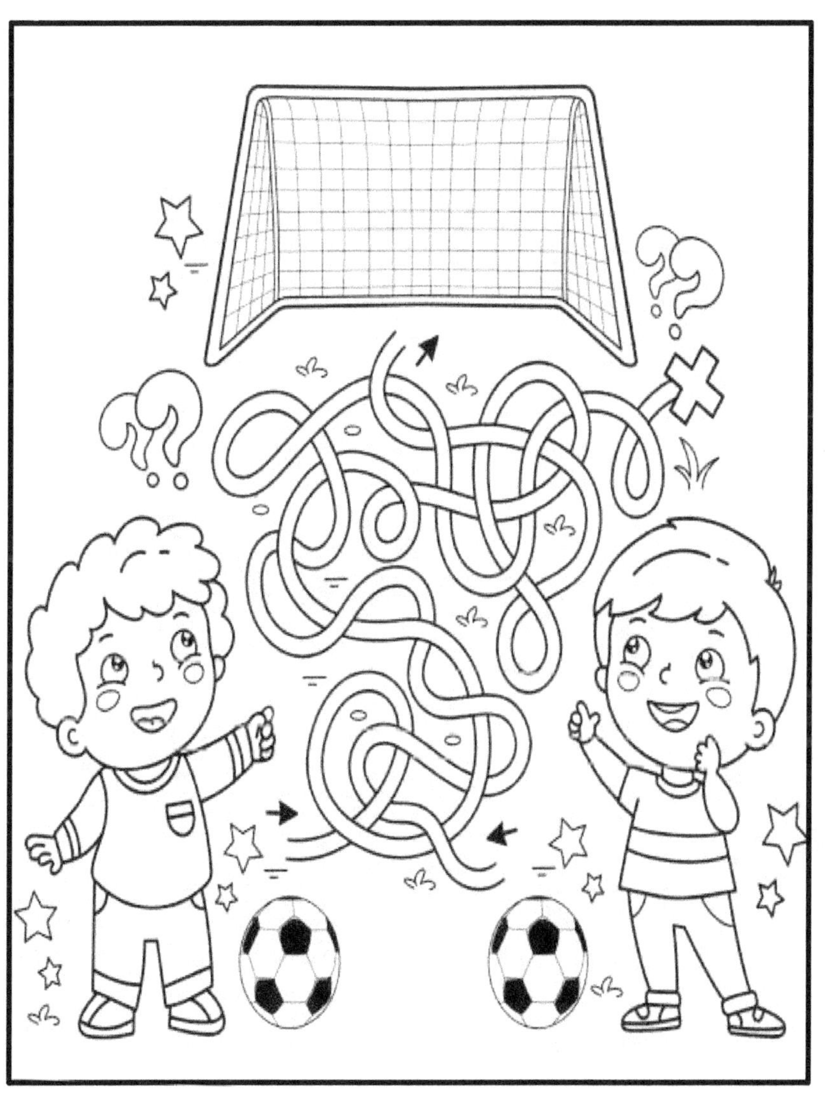

Color the picture and guess Who will score a goal in the gaol?

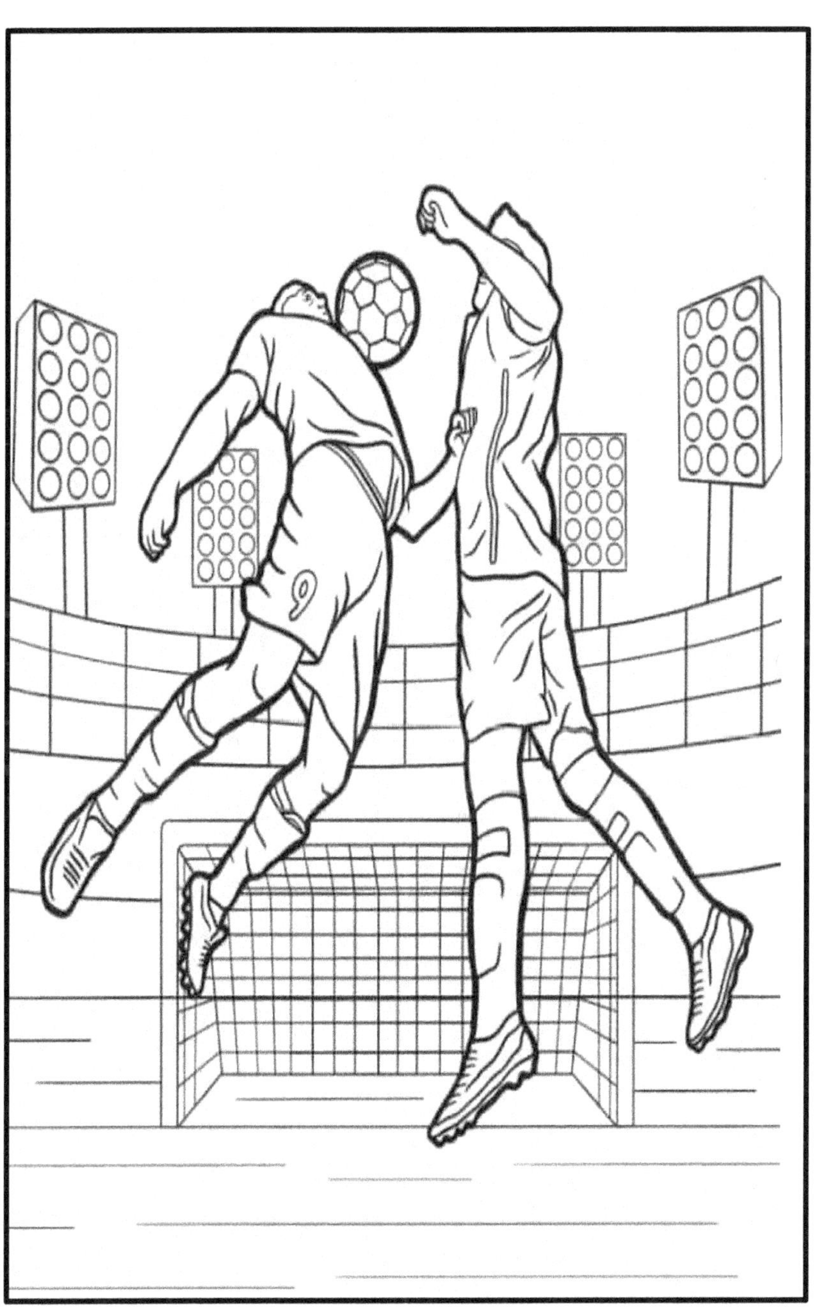

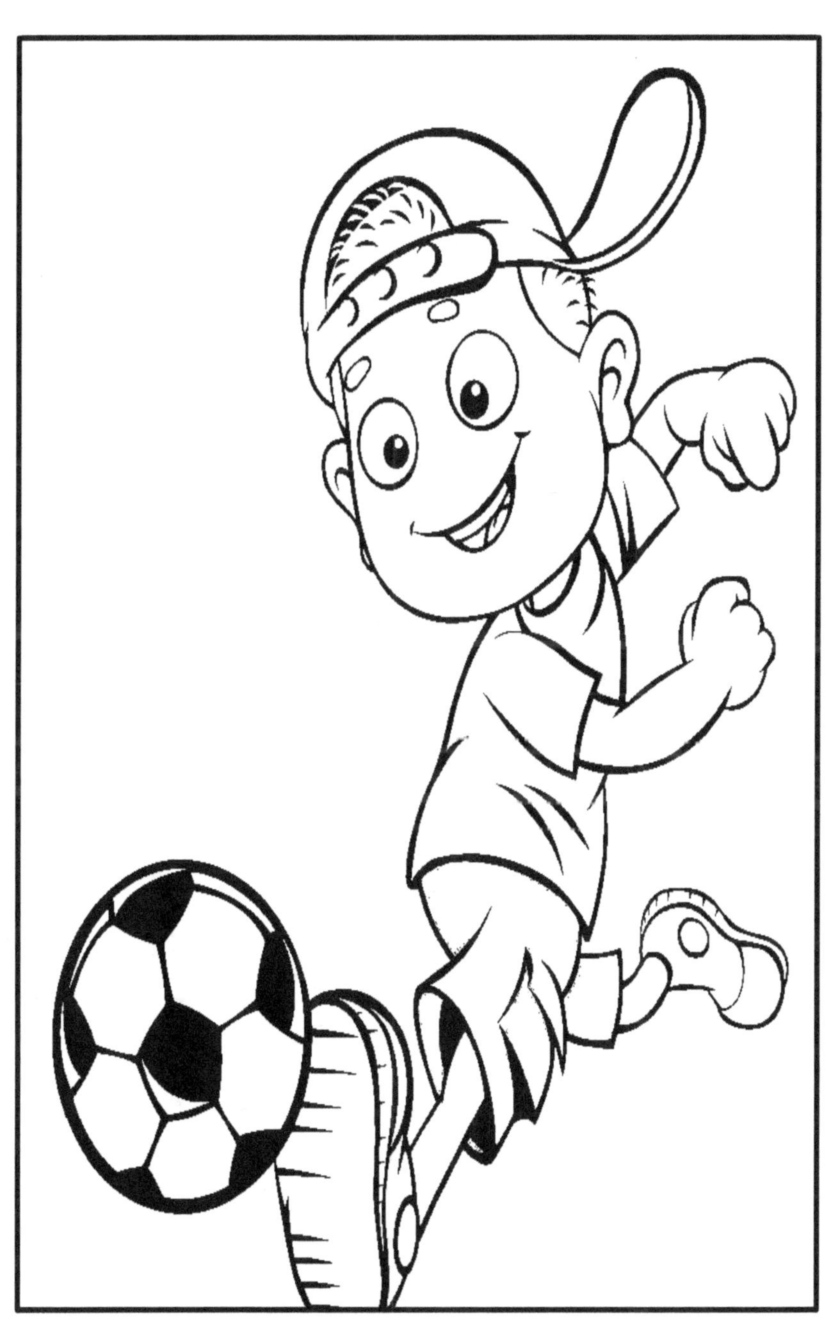

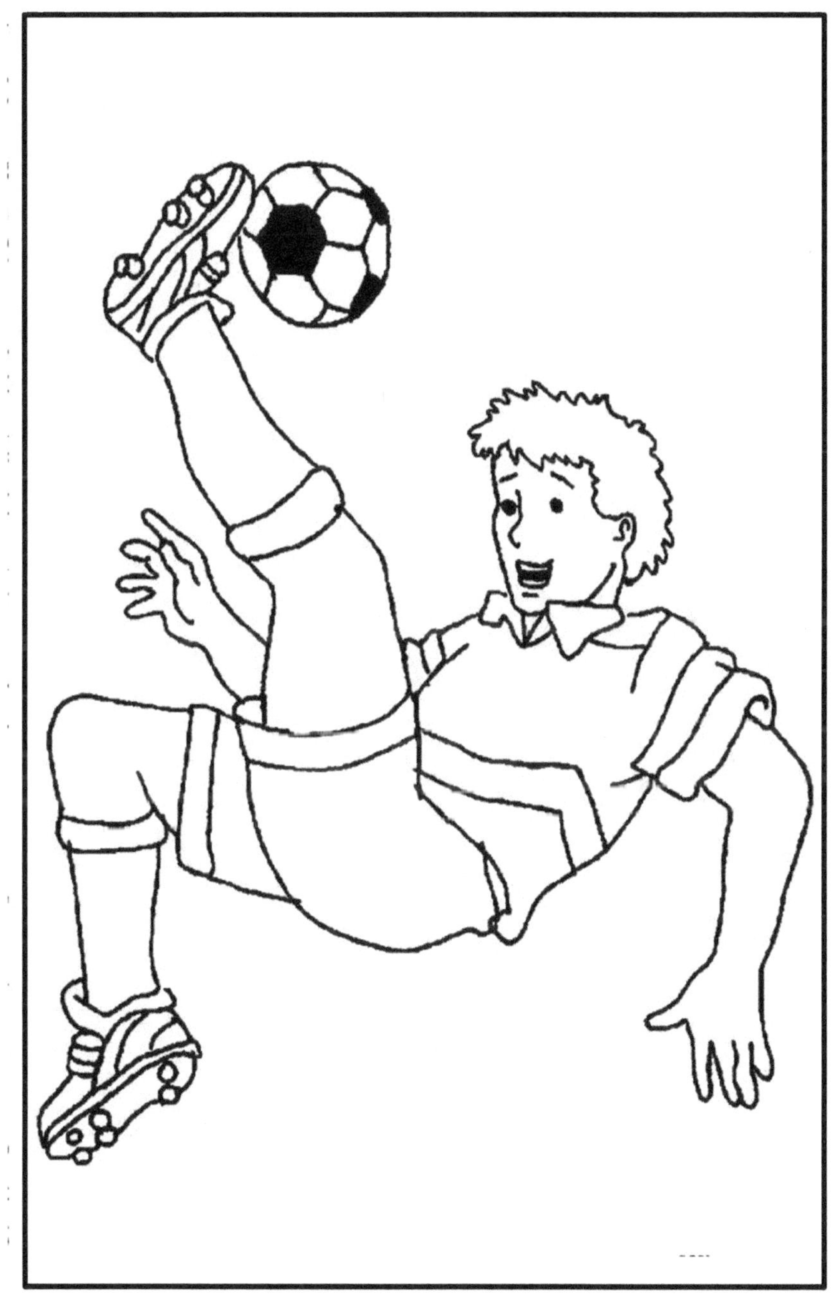

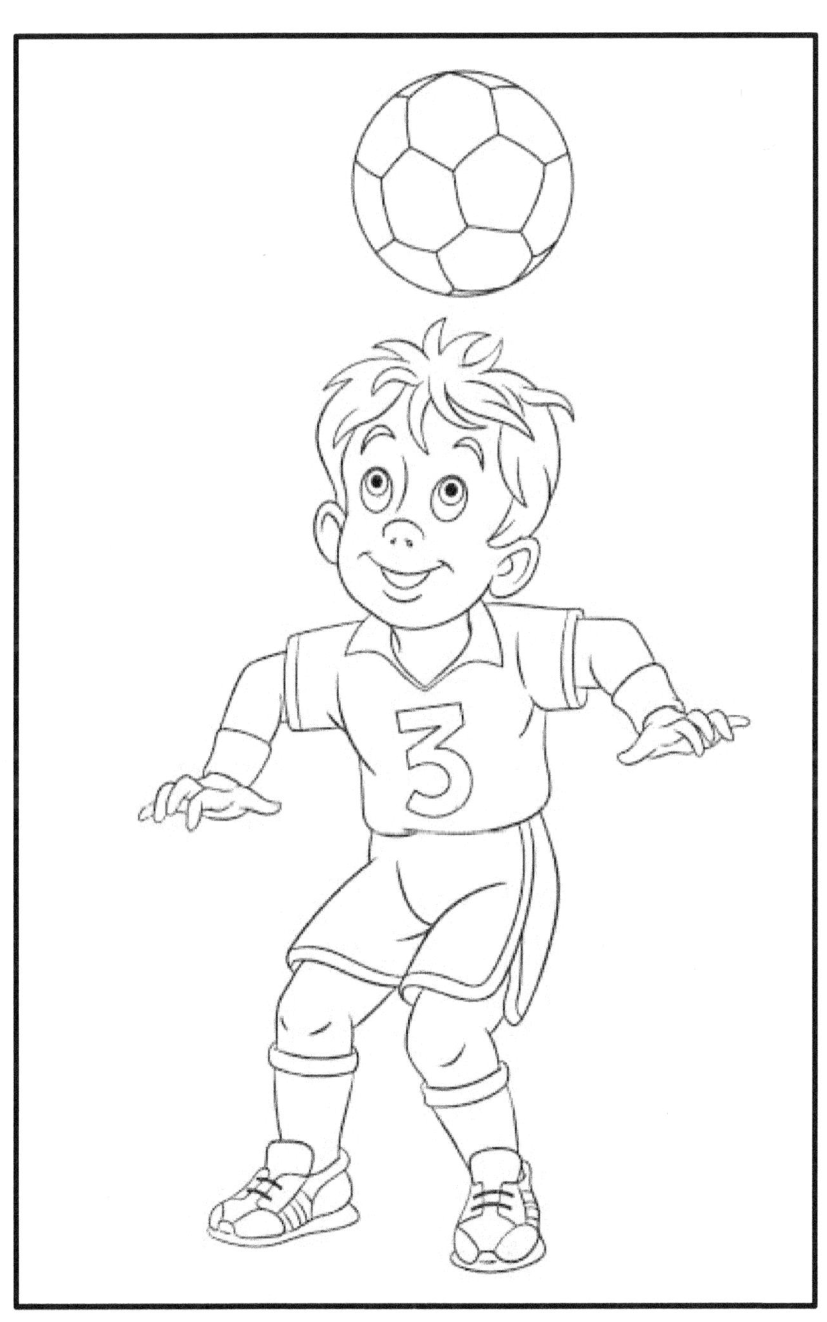

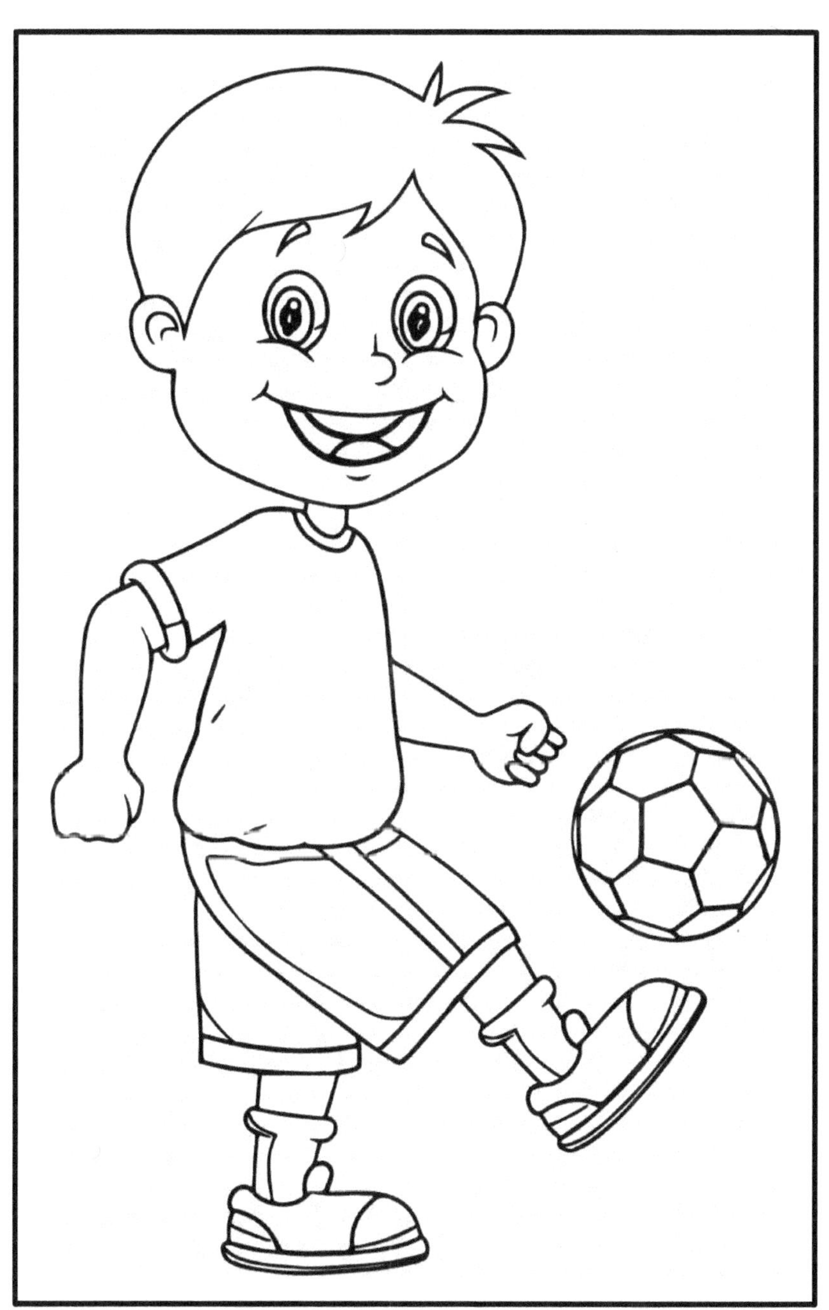

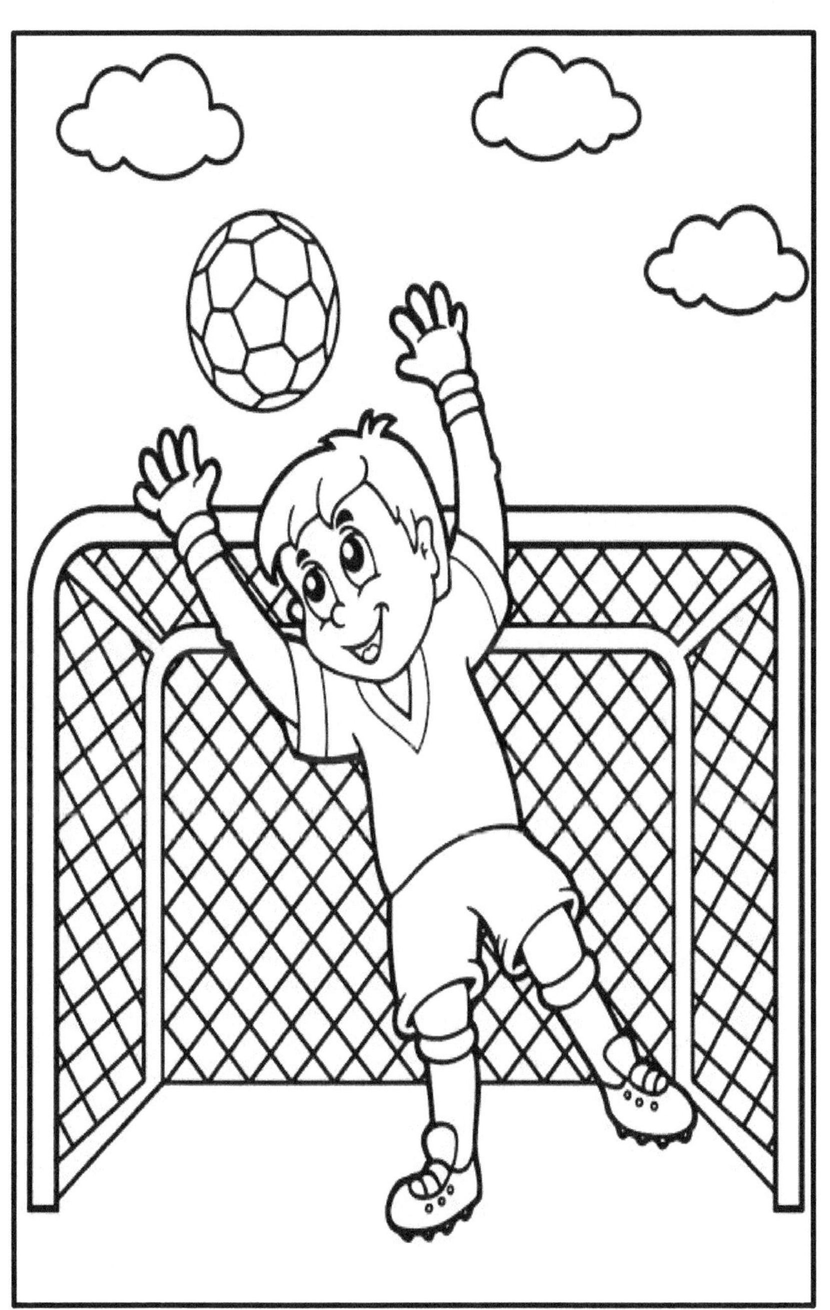

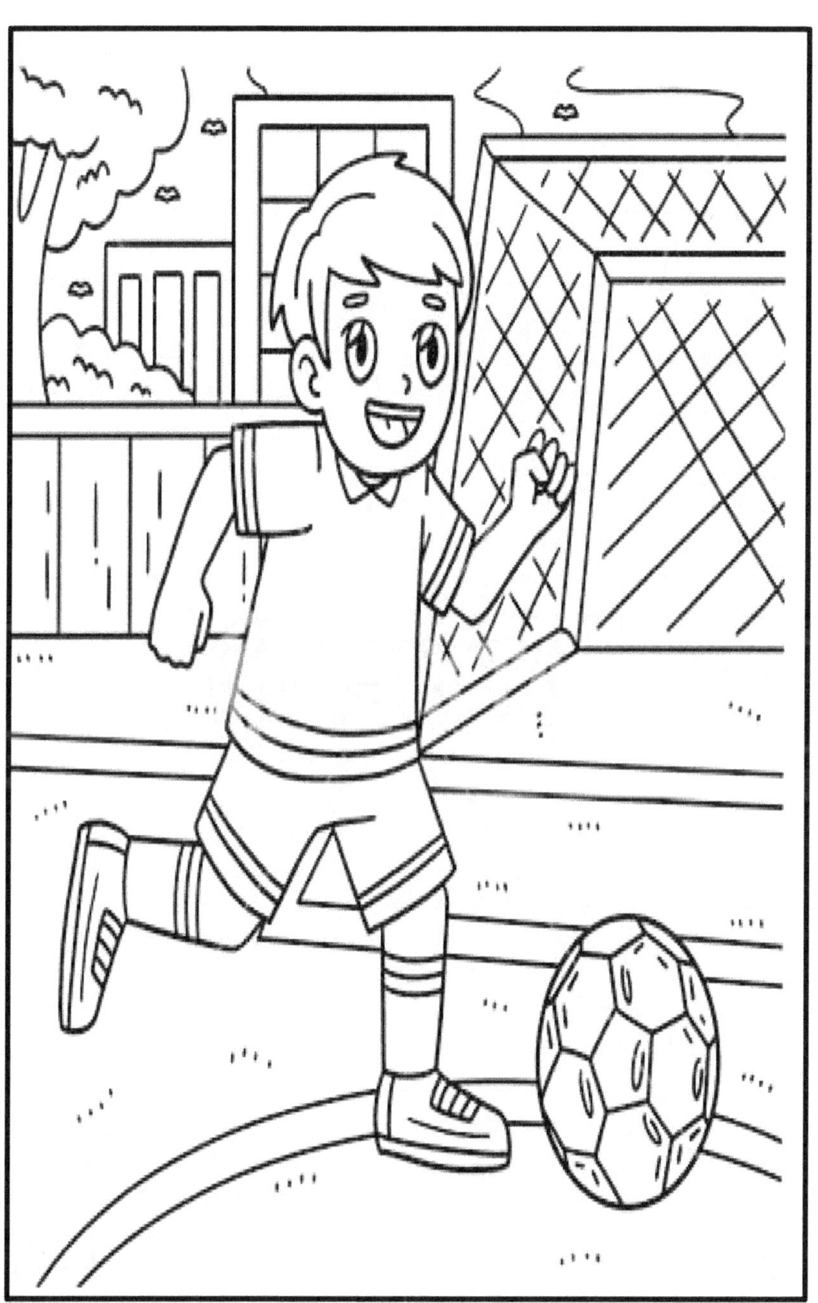

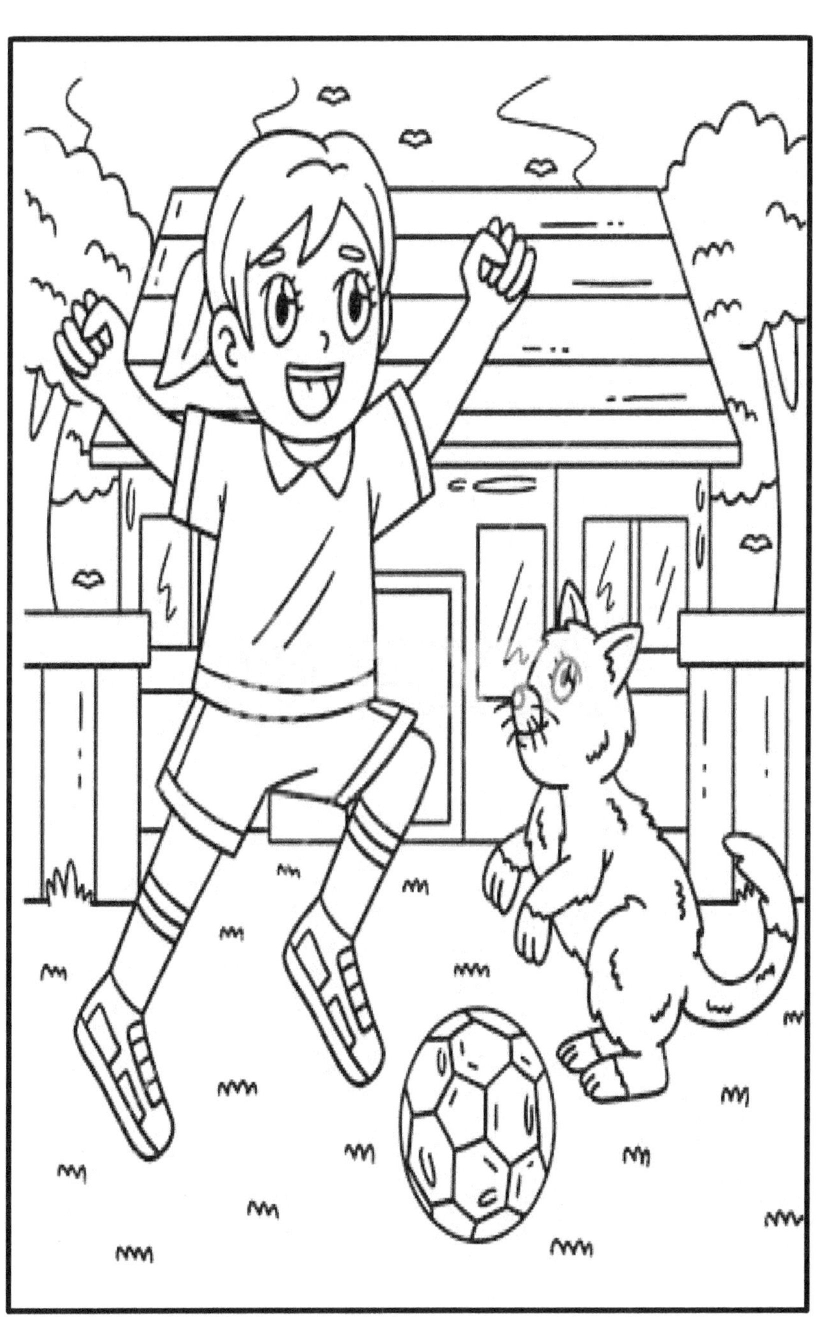

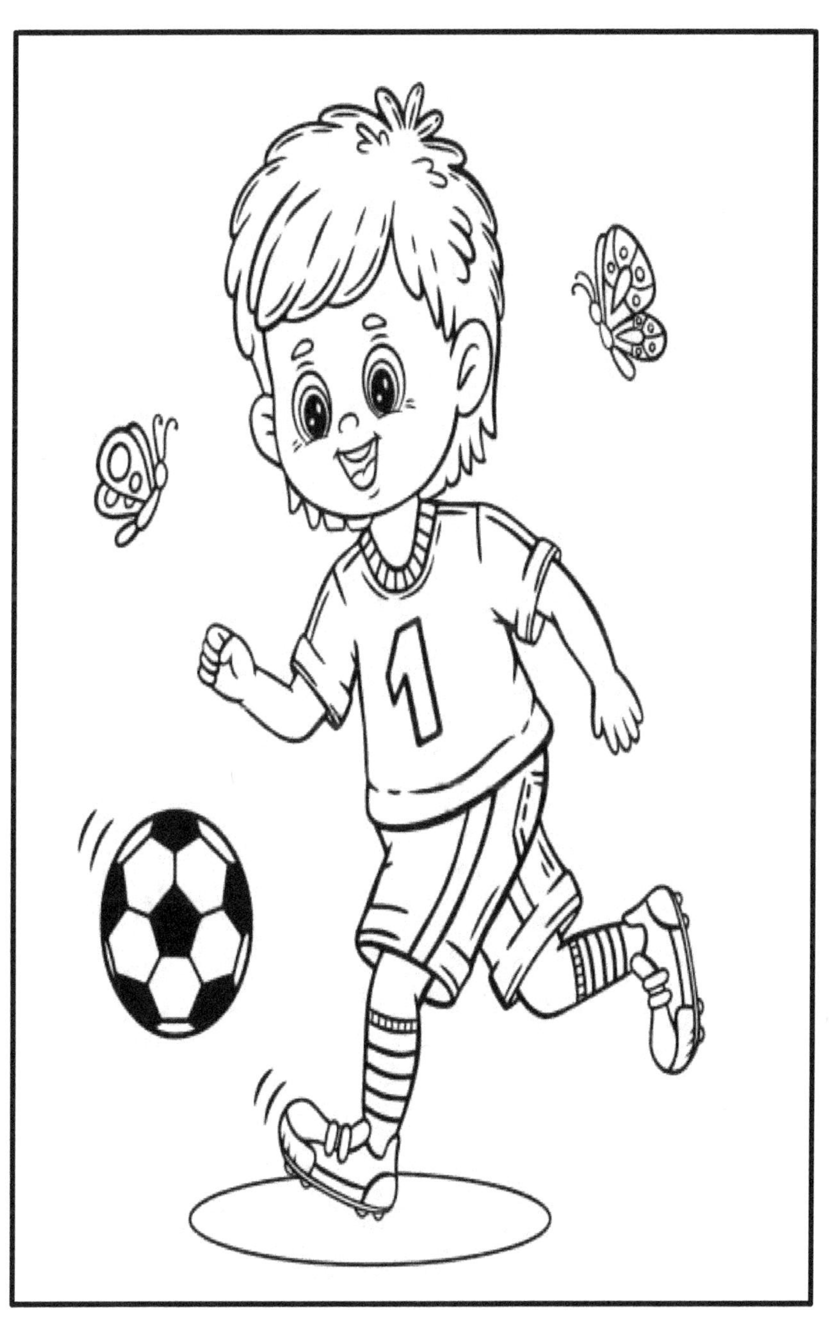

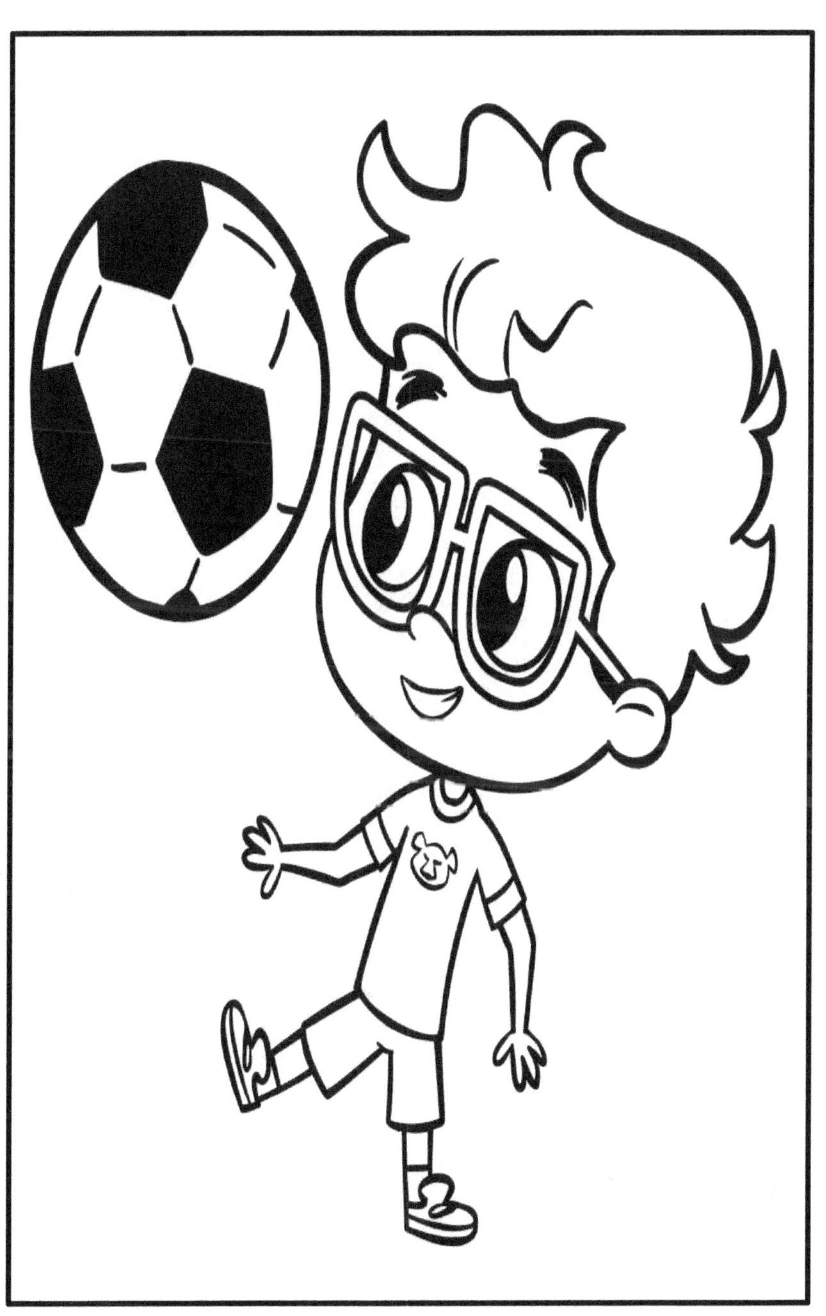

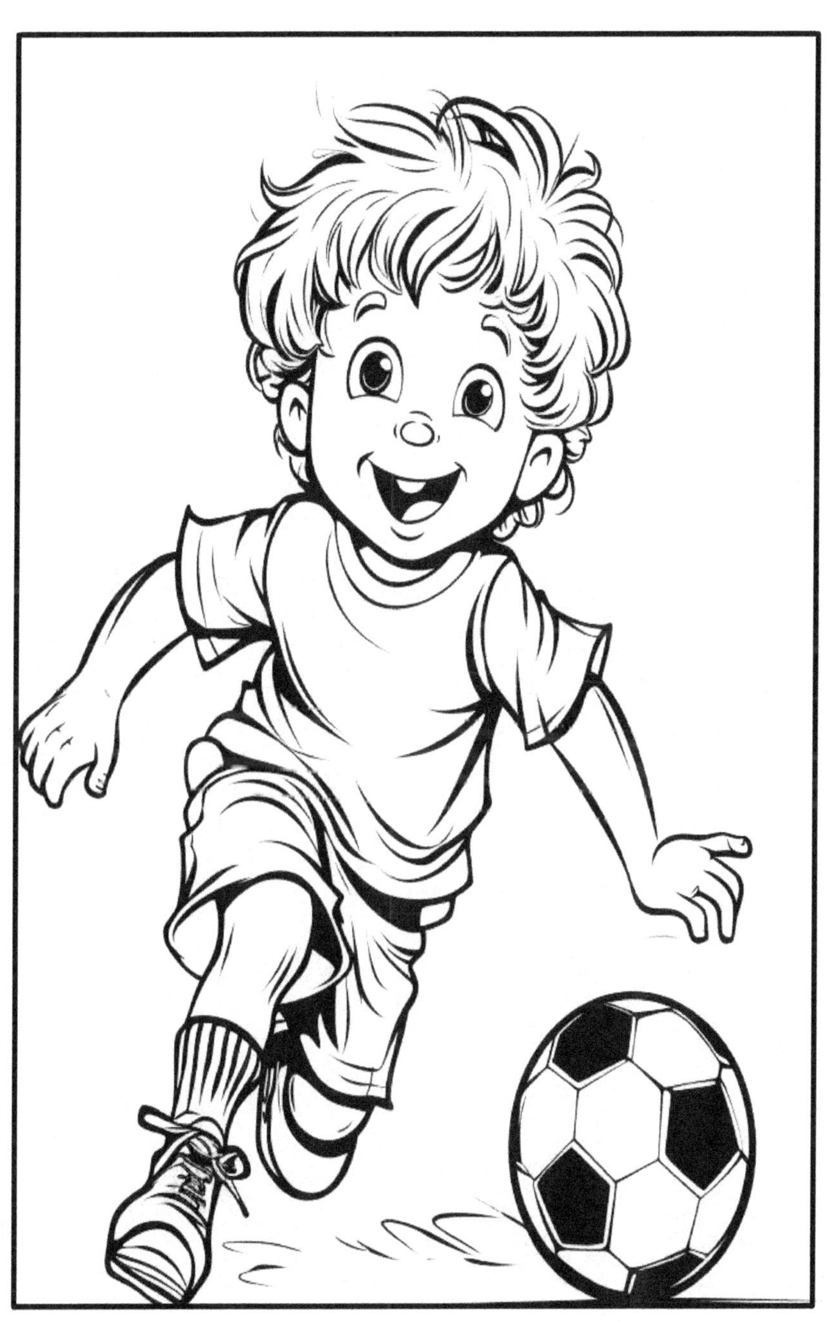

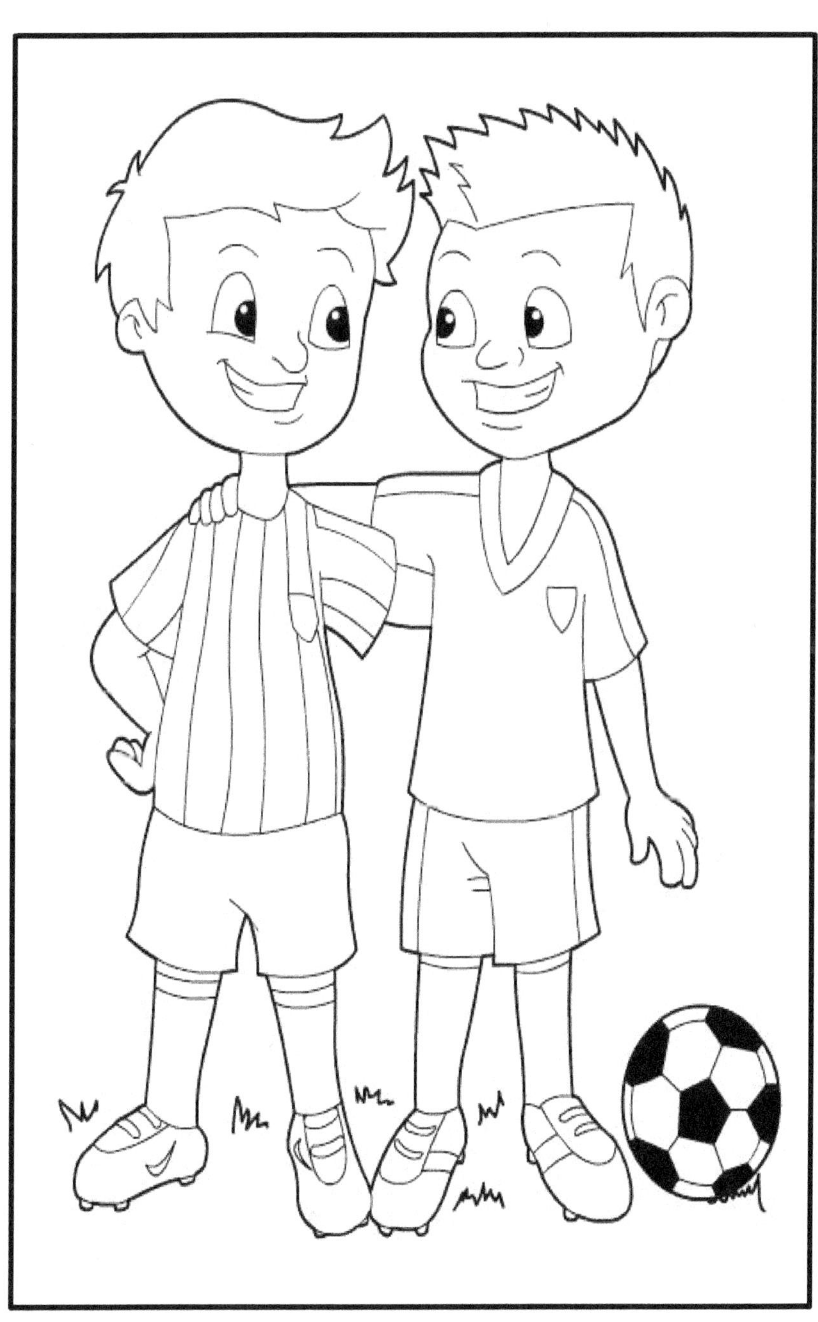

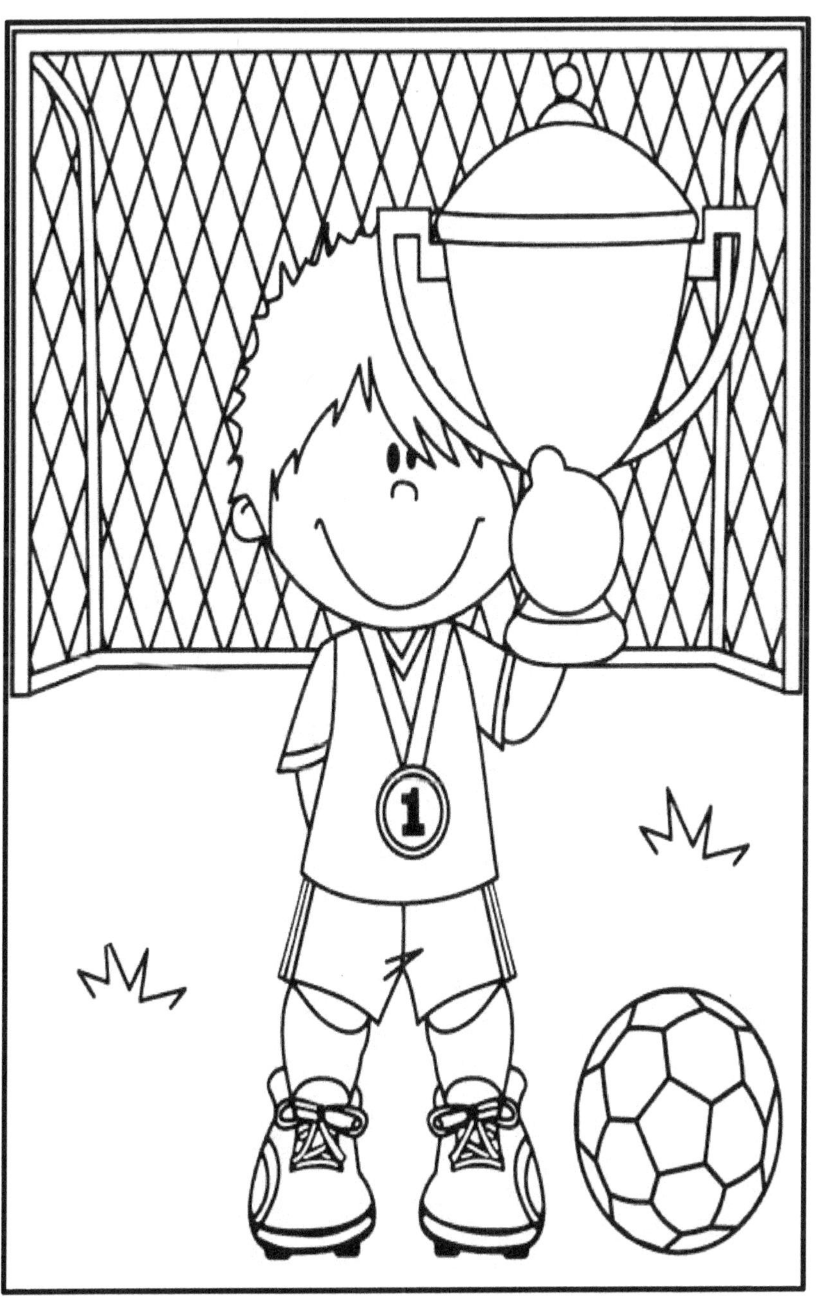

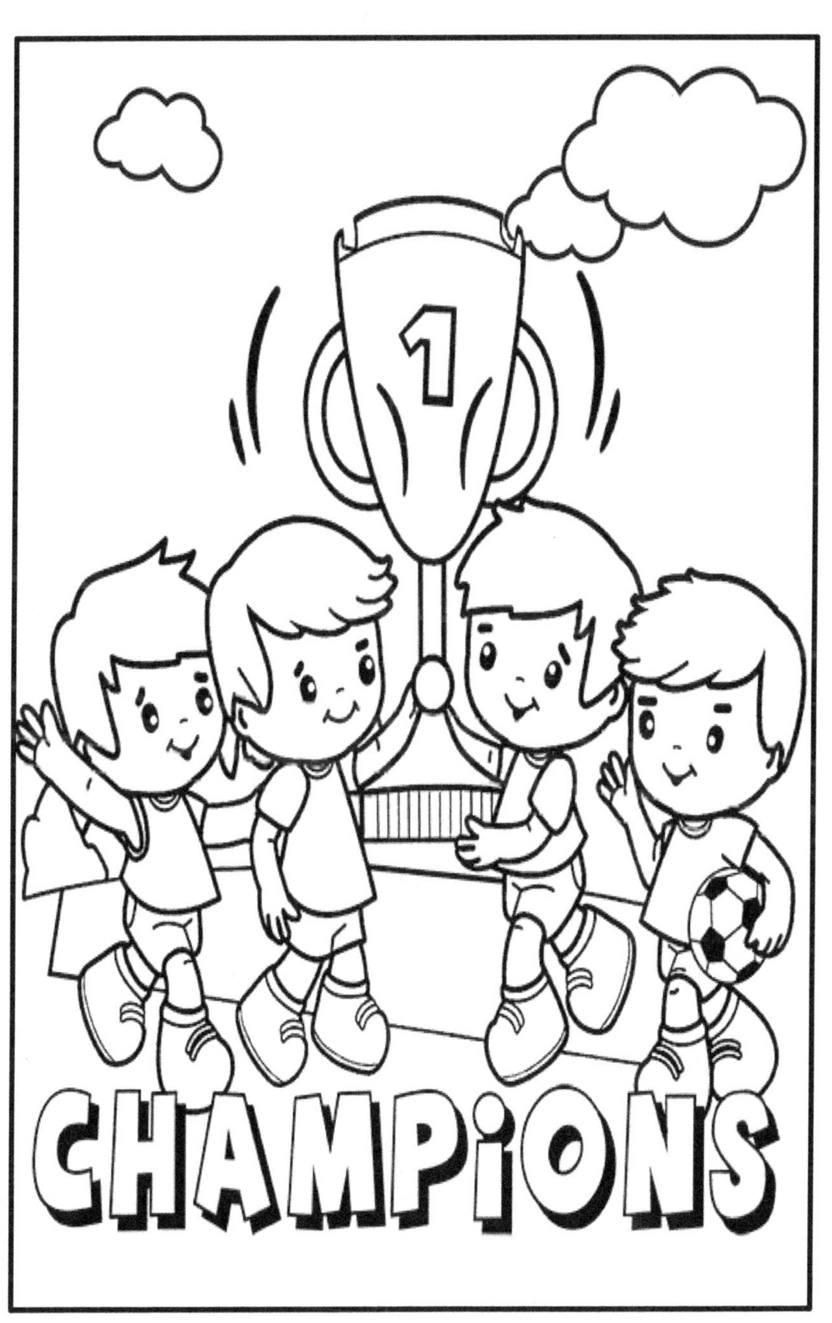
CHAMPIONS

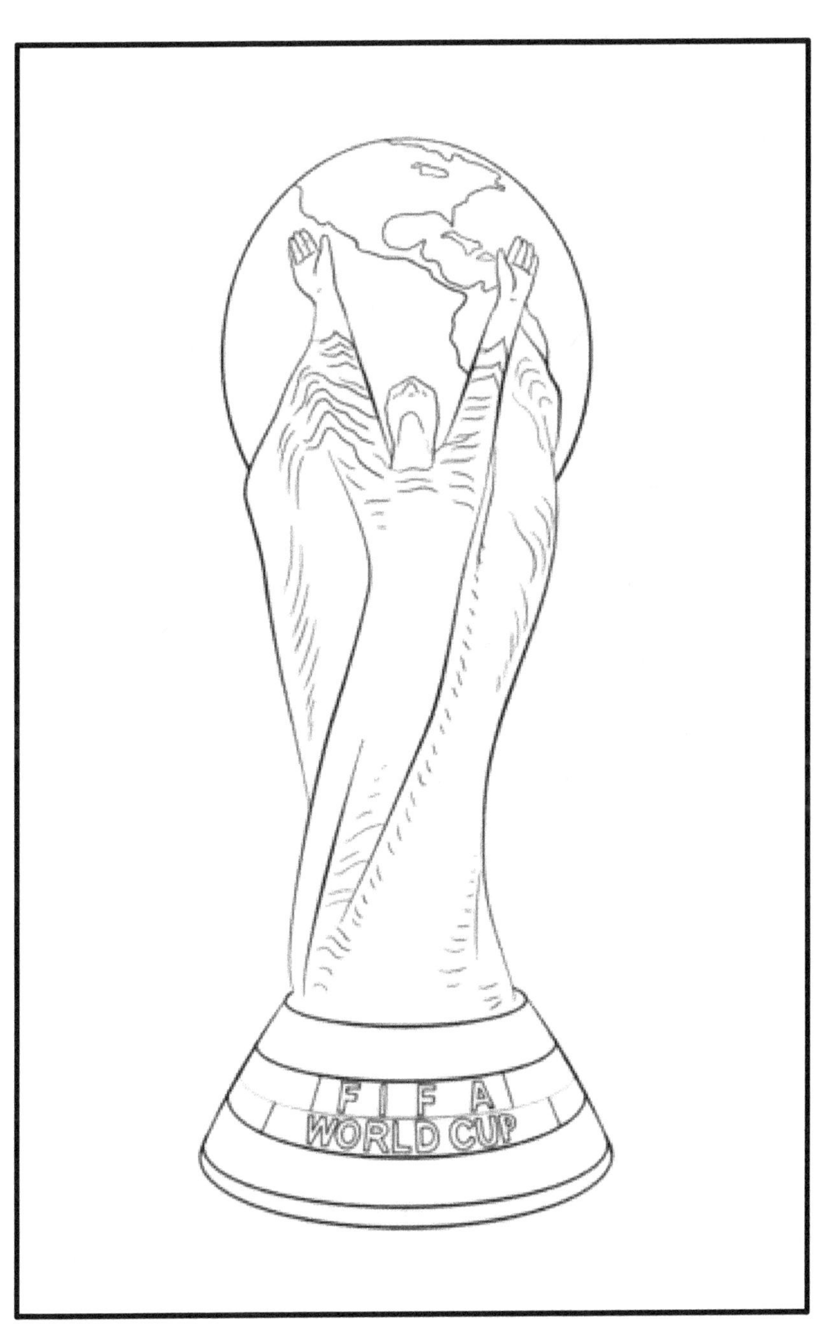
F I F A
WORLD CUP

YOU ARE THE

WORLD CUP

CHAMPION